Contents

Our Long Struggle for Home

Our Long Struggle for Home

The Ipperwash Story

Aazhoodenaang Enjibaajig

(THE ONES WHO COME FROM
AAZHOODENA)

on
point
PRESS

VANCOUVER | TORONTO

31 30 29 28 27 26 25 24 23 22   5 4 3 2 1

Printed in Canada on FSC-certified ancient-forest-free paper (100% post-consumer recycled) that is processed chlorine- and acid-free.

Library and Archives Canada Cataloguing in Publication

Title: Our long struggle for home : the Ipperwash story / Aazhoodenaang Enjibaajig (The Ones Who Come From Aazhoodena)

Description: Includes index.

Identifiers: Canadiana (print) 20220265631 | Canadiana (ebook) 20220266433 | ISBN 9780774890571 (softcover) | ISBN 9780774890595 (PDF) | ISBN 9780774890601 (EPUB)

Subjects: CSH: Ipperwash Incident, Ont., 1993- | LCSH: George, Dudley, 1957–1995. | CSH: First Nations—Land tenure—Ontario—Ipperwash Provincial Park Region. | CSH: First Nations—Ontario—Ipperwash Provincial Park Region—Claims. | CSH: First Nations—Legal status, laws, etc.—Ontario. | CSH: First Nations—Canada—Government relations—1951– | CSH: First Nations—Ontario—Ipperwash Provincial Park Region—History. | LCSH: Race discrimination—Ontario. | LCSH: Ontario—Race relations. | LCSH: Ontario—Ethnic relations.

Classification: LCC E99.C6 O97 2022 | DDC 305.897/333071327—dc23

Canadä

UBC Press gratefully acknowledges the financial support for our publishing program of the Government of Canada (through the Canada Book Fund), the Canada Council for the Arts, and the British Columbia Arts Council.

On Point Press, an imprint of UBC Press
The University of British Columbia
2029 West Mall
Vancouver, BC V6T 1Z2
www.ubcpress.ca

Dedicated to the elders who led the way

DANIEL and MELVA GEORGE,
PEARL GEORGE, ABRAHAM GEORGE,
ROSE MANNING, CLIFFORD GEORGE,
and NELLIE ROGERS

"Stoney Point: It's part of us. It's who we are. It's in our DNA; you can't deny it."

– Kevin Simon

"This is where I was supposed to grow up."

– Cully George

Foreword

This book tells a treaty story and shows that treaties are living agreements. They are not merely one-off events – in 1764, 1827, or whatever the case might be. They are about relationships. Through time, their principles must be continually renewed. If there is a departure from the treaty path, its values should take the parties back to talking with one another and sharing gifts, as happened in the early treaty processes. And so this book contains a treaty story; first, because of the community's starting point: the Huron Tract Treaty of 1827; second, because of departures from these agreed upon beginnings; and third, through the Stoney Point peoples' efforts to link arms together, just as the older treaties promised and depicted in the wampum belts often accompanying them. Treaty teachings are very strong in this book.

As such, this work demonstrates to all Canadians the continuing relevance of our treaty relationships. Yet there is work to do. The treaty requires two partners, but Anishnaabe people are putting forward a treaty view while Canada and Ontario seem to dismiss this approach. Although there are moments of hope and possibility, the state too easily forgets the treaty's wampum rows and turns away from joining arms together, as represented in the Covenant Chain belt.

The tragedy of Dudley George's death is that he was acting with the understanding that the treaty relationship was real. Unfortunately, calls to link arms together in peace, friendship, and respect were denied at every level of Canadian society – from the state to the police.

It seems there is an assumption that there is something greater than treaties; an assumption that when Europeans arrived with their law, this law exclusively filled the space of legality and political legitimacy in the country. In this troubling view, treaties were a mere expedient to move Indigenous people aside so a so-called superior law could operate. This belief flows from the Doctrine of Discovery that holds that when Europeans first landed on these shores, their laws prevailed. The Europeans contained Indigenous governance and moved it to a smaller space. Therefore, when Dudley George acted on the treaty promises, the Crown disregarded their obligations to him and his community. While he and the others were seen as acting on something, it is regarded as a second order of law, if it is even recognized at all. Thus, under Canadian law, while the Anishinaabe people believe they have a colour of right to expect the fulfillment of the treaty, the Crown also believes they have a "colour of right" to override, ignore, or deny Anishinaabe laws regarding treaties. This allows the Crown to marginalize Indigenous Peoples and act as if the Crown has paramountcy or pre-eminence through parliamentary or court procedures. This is not linking arms together – there is no application of intersocietal law in this approach, which is one way the Supreme Court of Canada has described the interaction of Indigenous and Canadian legal perspectives.

Seeing treaties as creating intersocietal law, formed and sustained by two legal traditions, helps us understand that colour of right arguments run both directions. The challenge is to bring the parties back together to recognize one another's laws and synchronize them to produce peace for every living being in the treaty territory.

Treaties are a foundation for how we might relate to one another respectfully. They are not built on assumptions of inferiority, as occurs through the Doctrine of Discovery. They are about mutuality. They are about creating intersocietal law. They are about peace, friendship, and respect between peoples. Treaties should not be interpreted in ways that compel coercion; they are about persuasion. They are about dialogue. They are democratic. This is what it means to link arms together and search for mutuality and reciprocity. Treaties attempt to engage participation between First Peoples and those who arrived subsequently to form a country. The alternative founding law on the Doctrine of Discovery is not democratic. It is unilateral, and it is tyrannical because it is arbitrary from the perspective of those who were here first. Seeing Crown law as paramount does not recognize the value of Indigenous Peoples' law in forming (with others) how we live together in the past, present, and future.

I hope readers of this book will see that it is wrong to build our country on unilateralism, domination, and coercion. This is contrary to our country's democratic aspirations. Of course, this is also contrary to Indigenous Peoples' laws, relationships, and governance as well. For me, there is a choice: We could choose the Doctrine of Discovery path that takes us away from our highest aims. Alternatively, we could choose to see the treaties as a path to fulfilling our goals though ongoing invitations to sit down, talk with one another, respect each other's land and governance, and do so with principles and processes found in the treaties.

The two-row wampum belt showed that the Crown and Indigenous governments sail on the rivers of life with different vessels, but that we can also journey side by side in peace, friendship, and respect. The white rows of the two-row wampum belt that communicate these principles are about integration, measured separation, interdependence, and peaceful coordination. They are about finding harmony. They are about working together even as each party retains the ability to steer our own boats.

If we practice linking arms together, as depicted in the Covenant Chain belt, to create peace, friendship, and respect, this also reinvigorates Anishinaabe law. Disagreements within Indigenous communities must be attentive to *doodem* and clan teachings and not just Indian Act structures and common law traditions. Anishinaabe people could also apply their seven grandmother and grandfather teachings as they work through their differences of opinion. These teachings include *zaagidiwin* (love), *debwewin* (truth), *zoongide'ewin* (bravery), *dabaadendizowin* (humility), *nibwaakaawin* (wisdom), *gwayak-waadiziwin* (honesty), and *manaaji'idiwin* (respect). These principles have been woven into Anishinaabe constitutions, both oral and written, to guide Anishinaabe communities in dealing with their conflicts. Additionally, communities could look to their brothers and sisters of the Three Fires Confederacy and see how the Potawatomi, the Odawa, and the Ojibwe had different roles, coordinated roles, in working through difference. Anishinaabe people also have our ceremonial ways of connecting with one another to live in greater harmony and goodwill.

My point is that settling disagreements should not be stuck in a colonial cul-de-sac. Anishinaabe people can look to their own laws and legal processes to apply and create solutions to challenges we face. Moreover, Settlement Agreements with the Crown should be the means by which Canadian governments decolonize and recognize the importance of Indigenous law. Both Anishinaabe and inter-societal law should also be the means by which people decolonize in a contemporary setting within these territories. Again, these laws must be informed by the treaties.

This is actually honouring the pipe that solemnized the treaties and living into their teachings; living into the pledge, the covenant made to link arms together in peace, friendship, and respect. The pipe teaches us about lifting one another, encouraging one another as the smoke rises from its bowl. This symbolism unites two groups of people, the land, and the Creator.

I have often said that we cannot be reconciled with one another unless we first reconcile ourselves with the earth. Anishinaabe people have ancient relationships with the land that are mediated by our clans; we learn lawful behaviour from the bear, the otter, the pike, the eagle, et cetera. Our law is written on the earth. Our language, songs, and stories chronicle what we learn about living respectfully with the earth and the consequences that follow when we disregard the more-than-human world. When Europeans arrived, we invited them to live in harmony with our law, our social order, which took its cues or its standards and principles from the land. The Crown entered treaties with Anishinaabe speakers who linguistically organized their views around a dynamic, verb-based view of creation. The symbols chosen to memorialize these agreements include elements from the natural world.

The hope is that we see the land as a legal archive, a law library in a sense. When we learn how to reconcile ourselves with the earth, then our treaties (our relationships with one another) will be easier to reconcile. However, if we continue to ignore messages given to us by the pine trees and the sands and the waves and the birds, then we will find ourselves out of balance with one another – and with the earth.

Our treaties are to last for as long as the sun shines, the river flows, and the grass grows. If we do not take care of our relationship to the sun, air, water, and plants, we are not going to be around much longer. However, if we view ourselves as fellow citizens with the rocks, water, plants, and animals, we will realize that our treaties are not only between the Crown and Anishinaabe people. Our treaties are actually with the natural world that surrounds us. They are a covenant with the earth, reminding us to live in ecocentric rather than ethnocentric ways.

John Borrows

John Borrows is Canada Research Chair in Indigenous Law at the University of Victoria Law School. He is Anishinaabe and a member of the Chippewas of Nawash Unceded First Nation in Ontario, Canada.

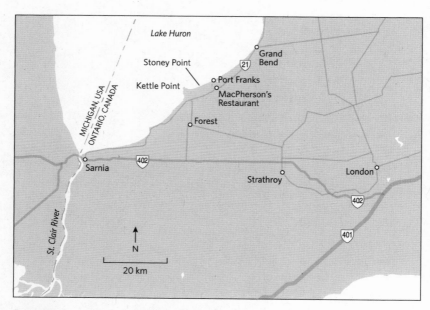

Stoney Point and Kettle Point, Ontario

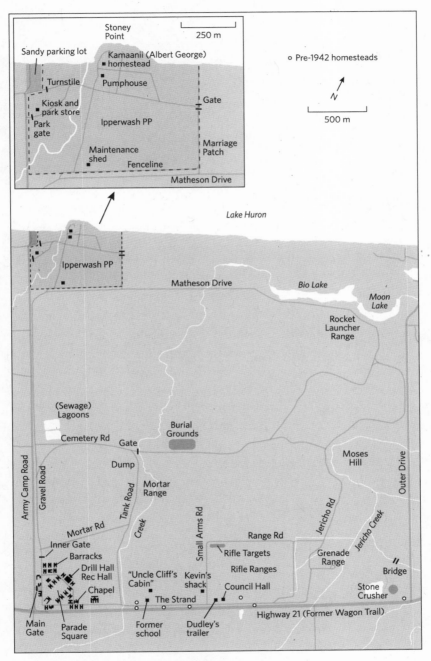

Ipperwash Army Training Camp and Ipperwash Provincial Park |
Kevin and Marcia Simon

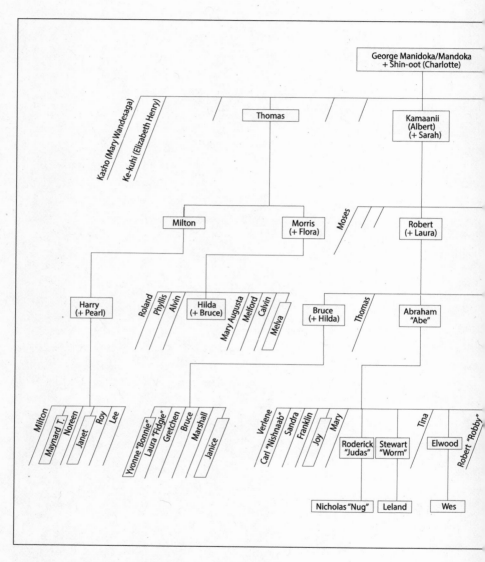

The George Family tree (partial) | Marlin and Marcia Simon
Note: The names that appear in boxes are those of individuals mentioned in this book.

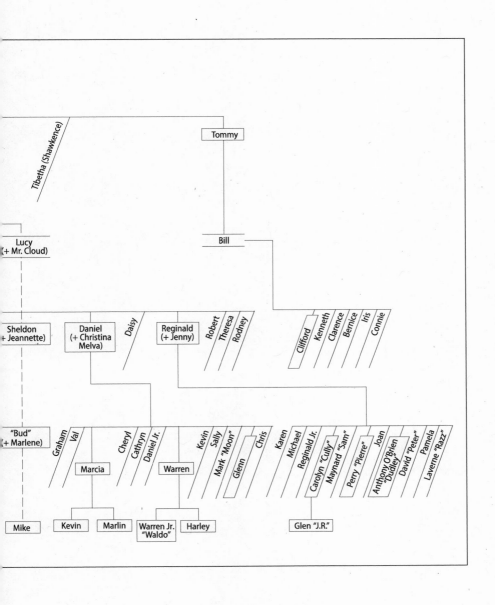

Our Long Struggle
for Home

Introduction

Twenty-seven years after Dudley George was killed on the night of September 6, 1995, we – the Nishnaabeg of Aazhoodena – are telling our story of what happened. We are telling it from our own perspective, in our own words, as much as possible. It's not just the story of an over-armed, racist police force opening fire on an unarmed group of Nishnaabeg trying to reclaim our ancestral homeland, one part of which had become the Ipperwash Provincial Park. It is the story of our way of life having been all disrupted when we were forced off the land that had given us life and shared identity for generation after generation – until 1942. Ever since, we have been trying to get back to that life, to our ways of living on that land. We have been trying to reclaim the land to which we and our ancestors belong, trying to renew that connection, that lived relationship, while we can still feel it strongly enough to act on it. To understand this is to understand something of our origin stories, our history and culture, including the culture of treaty making. And to do this is to share our hope that this country can be renewed in a good way, while justice is finally done here at Aazhoodena, the Stoney Point Reserve.

The reserve was created as part of the 1827 Huron Tract Treaty. Under that treaty, at least the "official" written version of it, between 2 and 3 million acres of rich, life-giving land in what became southwestern Ontario were "surrendered" to the Crown by the resident Ojibwe-speaking Nishnaabeg, including our ancestors. One million of those acres were given to the Canada Company to sell to prospective settlers. In addition, four large tracts of land, thousands of acres each and often on spots considered sacred, were set aside for the exclusive use of the Nishnaabeg for all time.

Together, these four pieces of land represented less than 1 percent of our former territory in this part of the Great Lakes (*Gichi-gaming*) watershed. Still, we were assured that this remaining land would be ours, for all time. One of these reserved areas was near what is now called Sarnia. Another is at Walpole Island on the shores of Lake St. Clair, close to Windsor and Detroit. Two tracts were bordered on one side by a long, curved stretch of fine-sand beach on the shores of Lake Huron north of Sarnia. One of these was called Kettle Point; the other, described as at the mouth of the River aux Sable, was Stoney Point. Our people had been living here for a long time already; we called it Aazhoodena, which means "the town across the way" (from Kettle Point). The Ojibwe word *oodena* means "a village," with "de," our word for heart, in the middle.

In 1942, the federal government invoked the War Measures Act to give itself permission to appropriate – to seize and take over – the entire Stoney Point Reserve. The government turned our land into an army training camp complete with rifle ranges, a grenade range, and another for launching mortar shells. It was understood that at the end of the war the land would be returned, but that didn't happen. Year after year, for decades, our people organized letter writing campaigns, petitions, and demonstrations, trying to get the government to honour its verbal promises, and the treaty as well. Regional and national Indigenous organizations got behind us and lobbied too. There was even a report by a parliamentary committee urging the land's return. But nothing happened. Canada's Department of National Defence (DND) maintained it still needed the land.

In 1993, six of our elders, including some of the last few who were born on Stoney Point, decided they'd had enough. They simply moved back home, and many of us who are their children came with them. Some of us had children of our own by then, and they came too.

At first, we lived in tents and trailers. One family's old hunting-camp tarps sheltered a shared eating area. As winter approached, we built more substantial accommodations, including small additions to some of the camper trailers where we could have a wood stove for heat. We built a council meeting hall. We revived our language and customs such as the sweat lodge and peacekeepers and tried to restore our self-governance traditions. Our actions drew widespread support from non-Indigenous groups and from other reserves, in the United

States and Canada. We hoped this would help advance a return of our land, but nothing happened. The government kept ignoring its promise, ignoring the treaty and the historical obligations associated with it. The army camp (now a cadet training camp) kept going, the barracks full. Cadets kept running around, learning to shoot rifles, grenades.

In 1994, the army shut down the cadet training camp, but not the base. They kept that going, with fewer soldiers around, but still they were there. A year later, on a Saturday afternoon in late July, we moved in on the barracks; that night, the army left the base. A few weeks later, at the end of the Labour Day weekend, some of us went a step further. We took over Ipperwash Provincial Park (by then closed for the season), a piece of the lakeshore that originally had been part of Stoney Point.

Newly elected Ontario premier Mike Harris decided to treat this as a law-and-order issue: these people were illegally trespassing in the park, he said, on land to which the province had legal title. Two days later, on September 6, there was a police boat patrolling offshore in the lake and a surveillance helicopter hovering overhead. Police were everywhere, and there were roadblocks on all the roads around us. In the moonlit darkness of that night, the combined forces of an Ontario Provincial Police (OPP) Crowd Management Unit plus a Tactics and Rescue Unit (TRU) – somewhere between thirty and forty officers – in full "hard tac" gear, shields, and visors, the TRU officers with semiautomatic weapons on their shoulders and guns in their holsters, and all with special issue steel batons swinging from their belts, marched down the road. In what happened next, they opened fire. Dudley George, a fun-loving guy, unarmed and dressed in sneakers, jeans, and a T-shirt, was fatally shot.

Dudley George was the only Indigenous person killed by the police in a land claim action (we call it a repossession) in the twentieth century. Stoney Point was the only reserve that has ever been taken over in its entirety and all of its people forced to move somewhere else. These are important things to know and each is a tragedy worth remembering. They are also part of a larger tragedy associated with what to us is a gaping hole in what has officially been called Canadian history. One of the biggest gaps is around treaties. They are the foundation of this country, lying underneath and coming before the 1867 Constitution. Anishinaabe legal scholar John Borrows calls them foundational constitutional documents.[1]

Most Canadians do not appreciate this,[2] but we do. All of us grew up knowing about the treaties, the two-row wampum belt – all those agreements about sharing the land that was given to us by the Creator, but also about retaining control of certain parts of our territory, our homeland, where we could continue our ways; could continue being Nishnaabeg.

John Borrows describes the treaties as "creating an inter-societal framework in which first laws intermingle with Imperial laws to foster peace and order across communities."[3] There are two important things in what he is saying here. One is that our (First Nations) legal traditions were the first laws of this land and were not extinguished by anything like occupation or conquest. So they retain their legitimacy, as affirmed in the treaties. The other is about the nature of these laws. They are diverse and entwined with the particular history and lived experience of each group.[4] Some are traditional or customary laws handed down from generation to generation through story and ritual and followed every day in our protocols and practices; our customary ways of doing things like hunting and harvesting medicines. Some laws are considered sacred, because they "stem from the Creator, creation stories or revered ancient teachings that have withstood the test of time."[5] Many of the first laws are also natural laws based on close observation of nature. They are laid out in the natural order of things, the mutuality of respect and of different species living together and understanding how the earth maintains functions that benefit all beings.[6] Potawatomi SUNY botany professor Robin Wall Kimmerer celebrates the grace and the beauty of this mutuality in nature's interconnectedness and interdependence: insect to plant, plant to plant and to human beings too – sweetgrass flourishing, for instance, where it is regularly picked and used. As she wrote in *Braiding Sweetgrass,* "My grandmother always said: 'If we use a plant respectfully it will stay with us and flourish ... This place always gives good sweetgrass since we tend to it right.'"[7]

The first treaties for sharing the land with newcomers from Europe go back at least to 1659,[8] and have their roots in diplomatic councils for peace and trade.[9] From long before then, but continuing since, treaties have not been primarily legal contracts. They were more like pledges and covenants, even sacred ones. "Because First Nations followed their own legal traditions in creating treaties," Borrows has written, "their interpretation was that treaties were made with the Creator as well as with the Crown."[10] Treaties created relationships;

ongoing relationships. These relationships were formal and political – setting down principles for "'constituting' their relations."[11] At the same time, treaties were also deeply personal. They were understood as between kin.

They were formally entered into with the exchange of gifts – such as wampum belts in our tradition; medals, clothing, tools, and sometimes liquor on their side. These "sealed a pledge to share space, creating a negotiated relationship as much as an economic transaction."[12] The relationships linked together the people who shared a territory over time. They also bound these people in an ongoing relationship with the land itself. The treaties were about sustaining this shared territory, the habitat, and all its inhabitants together.

The ongoing nature of the treaty relationship meant that the treaty also needed to be renewed on a regular basis, beginning with condolences, restitution, and reparation. These rituals and actions helped to restore balance and peace in the relationship. They set it right again.[13] That is how the treaty was renewed. For us and our way of thinking, this has not changed. The mutual responsibilities are ongoing, generation after generation, and shared by all.[14]

So we want to say miigwech to Heather Menzies, who showed up four years ago saying that the same 1827 treaty that had set aside the Stoney Point Reserve as our exclusive territory had also legitimized her great-great-grandparents being able to settle nearby. In 1832, her father's mother's people, the Crerars, bought land from the Canada Company. Ten years later, James Menzies bought a 100-acre lot from the company too. When Heather showed up, literally at the barbed-wire fencing around the old army camp, she said she had been learning about treaties from our point of view. She understood that they are relationships that must also be renewed, and she wanted to learn more, to learn what her responsibility might be. She said she had come to at least express her condolences.

We invited her in. We got to know her; she got to know us – and our dogs, too. She seemed sincere and compassionate. One or two of us had been hoping that someone with journalistic skills might come along to help us tell our story. We felt we could trust her to play that role. She became our writer assistant.

We drove her around. We gave her things to work with: photos; an old map; a history of our community, Aazhoodena, written by Daniel George's son Graham for the Ipperwash Inquiry into the shooting death of Dudley George. We directed her to the witness transcripts from the Inquiry: ours and others. She also taped our stories and took lots of notes. After nearly two years of visiting, sometimes for two weeks at a time, she set to work writing a first draft, then sent it to us to review. Draft followed draft with additions and changes according to what we wanted. There is one chapter that we mostly left to her to shape. This is Chapter 8, where she suggested we switch the point of view in the book to the police and government officials making decisions and taking action.

We also want to say miigwech to John Borrows who has honoured our story with his Foreword.

In helping to frame our stories in this book, we are grateful for the work of the many academics whose work we mention, many of them Anishinaabeg. We are also grateful for the work of the Ipperwash Inquiry (2004–07) and for Justice Sidney B. Linden who headed it. In his four-volume report, he created a written record of what happened and made all our witness testimony at the Inquiry publicly available. He also commissioned some important background research, including by Anishinaabe legal historian Darlene Johnston. We draw on it too and are grateful for it. We also pulled in material from our own personal files. Some of these are documents that other family members have written, others were commissioned by the band office. These tend to be photocopies stapled together or assembled into a three-ring binder. They are not officially published books but important sources nonetheless. We also draw on the deep memories each of us has, not only from the events of the 1990s, but from childhood and the stories handed down to us growing up.

Some final words of thanks: first, to Anishinaabe literary agent Stephanie Sinclair, for championing our story and helping us find a publisher; second, to Susan Abramovitch and Laurent Massam, partners with the Toronto office of Gowling WLG (Canada), who negotiated a publishing contract for us, and whose excellent services were donated through Pro Bono Ontario, which we also thank.

Chapter 1 begins with some oral history, drawing on memories and stories to sketch in a sense of how we lived our daily lives at Aazhoodena, the Stoney Point Reserve, before the army took over our homeland. We then step back to offer a brief history of how our people came to be in this place and the origin myths that tell us that we belong here. Then the Europeans started to intrude, drawing more of our people and the animals on which we depended into their fur trade, drawing our forebears further into treaty making as more newcomers came, wanting land on which to settle. After Confederation, we were drawn more and more tightly under the control of the federal government with its residential schools, its Indian Act, and its local Indian agents.

Chapter 2 continues with more memories; this time, from the day the army came to take our land. They moved some of our houses and destroyed others, as well as our barns, our gardens, and our root houses. They relocated some of us to Kettle Point and left the rest of us scattered wherever.

Chapters 3 and 4 cover the period from 1945 to 1990, providing brief histories of the key families involved, showing the damage that the disruption, the dispossession, and the dislocation inflicted – but also the persistence of our dream of returning home.

Chapter 5 recreates key moments in time from that first May morning in 1993 when a group of Nishnaabe elders, all of them now in the spirit world, brought folding chairs and a picnic lunch onto the army training camp in a first act of returning home. Chapter 6 chronicles more of what we did to restore our traditions and rebuild Aazhoodena, and also our walk to Ottawa, seeking recognition. Chapter 7 describes the takeover of the barracks and evening of September 4, 1995, when a handful of mostly young people extended our land reclamation action to include the Ipperwash Provincial Park once it was officially closed for the season. They put tobacco into the fire they had lit to honour the ancestors buried behind some of the sand dunes, happy that they were finally able to do this.

In Chapter 8, we switch perspectives. We draw on what Justice Sidney B. Linden wrote in his report on the Ipperwash Inquiry, plus witness transcripts, to recreate the two days leading up to Dudley George's death through the words and actions of the OPP and the government officials involved.

Chapter 9 brings the point of view back to us, the Nishnaabeg. We had carried on, unaware of all the government meetings and police planning, but getting more and more nervous at seeing more and more police around. Moment by moment, this chapter recreates the day of September 6, and in the darkness of that night, the firing of the high-powered bullet that killed Dudley George.

Chapter 10 covers the hours and days after the shooting, with all signs suggesting that the tragedy not just of Dudley George's death but all that lies behind his death would continue, the core issue unresolved. Very little has changed.

The penultimate section of the book, the Epilogue, begins with a brief update on what has happened since 1995, plus our vision for the future. It is followed by an Afterword by Heather Menzies where she describes how getting to know us has challenged her to change.

All of us sharing our stories here are related to each other, which is normal since kinship is the heart of Nishnaabeg life. But within this, many of us are descendants of four ancestors: Waapagance, Oshawanoo (Shawnoo), Pewash, and George Manidoka (Mandoka). Waapagance was chief of the Chippewas at Aazhoodena when the colonial authorities were pushing what they called the "Huron Tract" treaty talks in the 1820s; Oshawanoo was a nephew of Tecumseh whose sister, Tecumbeesh, fled north and east with Oshawanoo and another son in the first decade of the 1800s after their Shawnee village was attacked by American forces. Oshawanoo married Mashankegahsenoqua, daughter of Pewash, who was one of the earliest chiefs of the Chippewas of Kettle Point;[15] George Manidoka fled the United States with his wife Shinoot (Charlotte) and their children, along with other Potawatomi to escape "The Trail of Death" after US president Andrew Jackson signed the Indian Removal Act of 1830, forcibly relocating the Potawatomi, the Cherokee, and other nations from territories east of the Mississippi to the west of it.[16] For the Potawatomi Nation, this meant being displaced from Indiana to Kansas. Some of the refugees settled in Aamjiwnaang (Sarnia); some in Bkejwanong Territory (Walpole Island). Mandoka and his family eventually settled in Aazhoodena.

Janet Cloud, Maynard T. George, Gina Johnson, and Bernard George are descendants of Waapagance. Tom Bressette, Rosalie (Rose) Elijah Manning, and Melva and Hilda George are descendants of the Shawnoo family; though Hilda's father and Melva's grandfather Morris was a grandson of George Mandoka. (When the Mandoka family was baptized in 1860, the authorities dropped the Indigenous name, which signifies a "being with spiritual power," leaving George as the family name.)

One of Mandoka's sons was Tommy, and one of his grandsons was Clifford George. Another of Mandoka's sons was Kamaanii, also known as Albert. Albert George, in turn, had six children, including Robert, whose own children included Reginald, father of Dudley, Pierre, and Cully; Daniel, father of Marcia and Glenn; and Bruce, Bonnie Bressette's father.

Thomas was another of George Mandoka's six sons. One of Thomas' children, Morris, had eight children, including Hilda, who married

Bruce George, and Melva, who married Daniel. Another of Thomas's sons, Milton, had several children and grandchildren, with one of the grandsons being Maynard T. George. (See genealogy chart.)

Finally, a few words about how others have named us, as well as what we choose to call ourselves and how we spell this to convey our own local way of speaking. The word Ojibwe or Ojibway is an anglicized version of a word the Cree used to describe the people living in the Great Lakes territories. Some even say Jibwe. Then there is Chippewas. The British often used that word to describe us, and now it is part of the Kettle and Stony Point's official Indian Act "band" name. In the 1980s, though, a lot of us, the people of the Great Lakes, began returning to the original word we used, which means "good beings" or "human beings."[17] In our language, this word is Nishnaabe. *Nishin* means "good"; *naabe* means "being." The word Nishnaabeg refers to us as a collectivity, a nation, while the language we speak and are trying to restore to living vibrancy is Nishnaabemwin.

We understand that the word "Indigenous" is used now to describe us in general. As much as possible, however, we identify ourselves by using more specific words such as Nishnaabeg or Haudenosaunee. When a more general word is required, we still tend to say "Native" and "non-Native," and so we'll often use that here. As much as possible, we're trying to stay true to how we talk and tell stories.

Throughout the book, we are using the *Eastern Ojibwa-Chippewa-Ottawa Dictionary* as our guide in spelling. It uses phonetic spellings that honour the particular pronunciations we give to different words here. Hence, Nishnaabeg instead of Anishinaabeg, which reflects how the word is spoken elsewhere. However, we will use other spellings, like Anishinaabe, if that is what others use themselves. We want to respect the variation in intonation and dialect from place to place.

We use an *e* in spelling Stoney Point to designate the original reserve but drop the *e* when referring to when they started calling us part of the Kettle and Stony Point First Nation.

In writing our story, we refer to our home community as both Stoney Point and Aazhoodena, sometimes interchangeably. Aazhoodenaang refers to us as the people who live here; this explains how we have described ourselves as the collective authors of this book.

We do not pretend to speak for all who call themselves Aazhoodenaang, from Stoney Point. "We" and the idea of this book began among the people who have carried on living on our homeland and others who worked hard to have our land returned and stayed living nearby, at Kettle Point.[18] From that nucleus we reached out to others, particularly the children and grandchildren of other elders who led the way. In bringing all of these voices and stories together in this book, we are trying to honour the elders' vision. Calling ourselves Aazhoodenang Enjibaajig, which is the name they gave to all the ones trying to reclaim our homeland, is part of that honouring.

CHAPTER ONE

No Word for Surrender

The elders who led the way home in 1993 didn't just know that Stoney Point was home as a historical fact. This knowing was embedded in their muscles and bones from having been born and raised on the reserve, steeped in its daily routines, the seasonal rounds of shared work; a Nishnaabe life and way of life that had evolved here since long, long before the Europeans came.

Clifford George: "We lived mostly off the land ... rabbits, racoons, muskrat, too, and deer. Morels and stuff like that first thing in the spring and then we started having strawberries. They were small but they were wild and they were good. And then raspberries, all the different kinds, and we had thimble berries, and it all grew wild and we used it and it just kept on going. I notice now that they're all dying off because it's not used ..."[1]

"We have an idea that the Creator put us there on account of all that we needed was there ... We have a very strong spiritual conviction about all that, that the land was spiritually given to us, many years ago ... That's why we're put on this earth. You are the keepers of the land, the Creator told us ...

"Lena Lunham, she's the one that brought me into this earth – this world. She was a great medical lady. She knew every plant that was in the bush that she walked through ... She knew every plant that was good for us, and also, she was a midwife for just about everybody. She didn't have to be told. She just walked through the bush. So when they saw Lena coming, they said, put the water on because here comes Lena. She'd be walking across a field, and it was just wonderful to see.

"The whole reserve was very close. Like, if we killed a deer, well, we split it with all the other people."

Lena Lunham was Rose (Rosalie Elijah) Manning's grandmother. Rose was nearly eleven when the army came, and she remembered a lot. "There were all kinds of things in the bush that you could survive on. All kinds of rabbits and small game like squirrels. And of course we had our farm too. We had a few chickens and we had one or two cows.

"I had my best years in Stoney Point. I went to school in Stoney Point. I went to church in Stoney Point. I also seen people that died and were buried there.

"I knew all the people there and I trusted all the people there and they trusted each other. You went to visit somebody, they'd give you a drink of water as soon as you entered their house – no matter what time of day or night. It was a sharing, caring community, but it was a small one."[2]

Others, born later and therefore much younger when they were forced off the land, have scattered memories – including of Laura George, who was a midwife in Stoney Point.

Marcia (George) Simon: "She was telling me how to make a homemade incubator if the baby is born a little early; you had to heat rocks. She was so smart; she knew all those things."

Theresa (George) Gill remembers Laura, her mother, "threshing her beans in a sack," the crackling sound of it as the dried bean shells broke open, the shushing sound of the beans that would become soup rubbing past each other in the bottom of the sack.

A niece, Janice Isaac: "I remember Grandma Laura, 'I'm goin' to the bush for my dyes.'"

Another niece, Bonnie Bressette, remembers her Grandma Flora's root house: "It smelled so good in there, the sage, all the medicines hanging from the rafters, the peaches, the apples ... You could go in there and there's big bins. They were filled with all your food for the winter." It was dug down into the earth about two feet, had logs up the sides and a dirt roof. Two pipes kept the air fresh inside by providing circulation. "Everything you counted on to live was in there" stored in black-ash baskets and bins.

"Your plants, your animals, your medicines, everything here depends on the land.

"To us, land is life. If you didn't have land, you would have no life ... Without land, you don't have no life."

Janet Cloud: "Our mum [Pearl George] told us a lot of stories; her and Grandma and Auntie Liz. They'd get a jar of tea and go back along the inland lakes there and they'd make up their baskets. The men would do the pounding and do the stripping of the [black ash] splits and Mum would make the baskets. And they liked taking their lunch back there. They would take salt-pork sandwiches in fry bread, and they would take little small jars of whatever they canned: peaches or pears or whatever. And their bottles of tea in the sealers. That was their lunch. And they took their time. It was so beautiful back there. They loved it there. They knew who they were. They knew who was true Stoney Point.

"It was a self-sufficient place where she lived. They had a barn. They raised pigs, and they had chickens, and they had geese. They had a little orchard, and they had two spring wells; really crystal clear. Mum said that that water tasted *so* good, and that was destroyed on our property.

"And they had a sawmill; they were the only ones with a sawmill. There was a fire on the reserve back then, and what the men did was they took all the burned timber [from the original log houses] and they sawed it all up and they began to make houses with that timber that they'd been able to salvage."

There were work bees for everything – making maple syrup, ploughing, and planting – and buzz bees too. For cutting up people's firewood, they used a circular saw powered by the power take-off of a tractor. There was no hydro, so most of the power was from horses, and many of us can remember them: workhorses with big hairy feet that people wrapped in old scraps of hide or sacking when they took them out on the ice in the winter. The horses helped with hauling ice in from the lake – and fish too, the nets strung under the ice. They helped drag logs out of the bush and plough everyone's gardens ready for planting in the spring.

The settled, cleared spaces remained small. Most of the reserve was left as it was: traditional hunting and trapping grounds where we also went to pick berries and to forage for walnuts, hickory nuts, butternuts, and for medicines and different things we used for dyes. These hunting and gathering grounds stretched for kilometres through land that had been left wild, its own self-determining place. The trees were a mix of species that had come to grow comfortably together in the long passing of time: walnuts and chestnuts, maple, black ash and birch, cherry, hazelnut and hickory, and massive oak trees, plus pine trees and sumac on the sandy, dune-hilled land close to the lake.

Kettle Point was valued for its flint deposits, as was Stoney Point. But our reserve was also the only source of ginseng around, and people would come from up and down the coast to get this precious medicine. They beached their canoes on the flank of sandy shore in the lee of the stony point itself, staying to visit with the members of the Midewewin society, medicine men and women. The crescent of sandy beach stretching from Kettle Point to Aazhoodena, with that distinctive stony outcropping at our end of it, was considered sacred by lots of people. It had always been known as neutral ground where people could make peace.

Bonnie: "People came to settle differences, knowing they were safe coming, they were safe leaving. You come in peace, you leave in peace." Bonnie was told this by an old medicine man, Peter O'Cheece, who also said: "Never let [this land] go. It is sacred land."

These are some of the stories handed down, the stories we commit to memory generation after generation.

HISTORICAL SKETCH

Through our stories we know that the Nishnaabeg of Stoney Point belong to the Three Fires Confederacy. This alliance dates a long way back; back to the prophecy of the seven fires and the great migration from the east when different tribes or nations,[3] all originating from the eastern part of North America, migrated into the lands of *Gichi-gaming* (the Great Lakes), including what is now southwestern Ontario. They shared a lot of similar Algonkian heritage, and this helped them in coming together as a confederacy. In the story that's told of how this started, three brothers, one from each of the three nations, met and forged the pact, with each responsible for a different fire in the alliance. The oldest brother, a Chippewa or Ojibway, was given responsibility to be Keeper of the Faith. He was to guard the spiritual knowledge of the three nations, recording their history and sacred/moral stories. The middle brother, the Ota'wa or Odawa Nation, was the Keeper of Trade. He was responsible for the economic well-being of the confederacy and also for preserving the sacred bundles. The youngest brother, the Ishkodawatomi or Potawatomi, was responsible for tending and safekeeping the Sacred Fire.[4]

For hundreds of years and well into the time of the fur trade with Europe, this confederacy controlled the territory around the Great Lakes. Its leaders negotiated relations with the Haudenosaunee (Iroquois) Confederacy, overseeing trade and maintaining the peace. Over time, the Three Fires Confederacy became the Great Lakes Confederacy, part of the foundation of what is currently known as the Anishinaabek Nation.[5]

The regional peace that these confederacies maintained began to break down when Europeans brought an ever-expanding commercial scale to fur trading across our territories. After a first contact with Samuel de Champlain near Georgian Bay in or around 1615, the Nishnaabeg generally allied themselves with the French, selling to them through our long-time allies, the Wyandot (Hurons), whose territory was concentrated around Georgian Bay. The Haudenosaunee, who were allied with the English, broke up this relationship in the 1690s during the Europeans' struggle for control of the fur trade.[6] There were more and more disruptions as fur sources disappeared because of overhunting. But there was more. Warring between the French and the English continued. And illegal freelance traders used rum as a trading commodity, bringing alcoholism as well as European diseases like smallpox into the area. And then the settlers came.

In 1763, Britain emerged the winner in its war against the French in the Americas, and France gave up its North American territories to Britain. When news of this reached the colonies in the spring of 1763, an Ota'wa chief called Obwandiac (called Pontiac by the English) called together a council of war with a view to pushing out all the Europeans, the English included. At least partly in response to Obwandiac's early successes that year, King George III issued his Royal Proclamation. It was a broad and sweeping promise of peace and ongoing recognition of our rights. First, it recognized our Nations as self-governing allies – although an added phrase "under Our Protection" undercut this with the contradictory idea that

British sovereignty could somehow override this.[7] It also promised to honour Indigenous title to any territory (referred to as "Indian Country" in the proclamation) beyond what had already been surrendered or purchased "by Us," (the Crown).[8]

The following year, the Crown's superintendent of Indian Affairs, William Johnson, set about turning the king's promise into the basis for a treaty. He sent out runners with invitations to a treaty council at Niagara, including to the Nishnaabeg of the Western Confederacy. The council brought together some two thousand chiefs and other representatives of twenty-four nations, not just from around the Great Lakes but from as far away as Hudson Bay and Nova Scotia, many of whom travelled for months to attend.[9] Johnson himself described it as "the most widely representative gathering of American Indians ever assembled."[10] It was hugely significant.

"The Royal Proclamation became a treaty at Niagara because it was presented by the colonists for affirmation, and was accepted by the First Nations."[11]

Lasting from July into August of 1764, the council served, in John Borrows's words, to renew and extend "a nation-to-nation relationship between settler and First Nation peoples."[12] The gathering dealt with many matters, including the exchange of gifts and prisoners, clarifying territory and forming new alliances. It also accomplished what Superintendent Johnson had hoped to achieve. This was a peaceful alliance between Britain and the assembled Indigenous Nations, allaying fears promoted, Johnson knew, by former French fur-trading partners that "[as] soon as we [English] became Masters of this Country, we should immediately treat them with neglect, hem them in with Posts & Forts, encroach upon their Lands & finally destroy them."[13]

Johnson related the promises in the Royal Proclamation to representatives of the nations gathered in the treaty council, "and a promise of peace was given by Aboriginal representatives and a state of mutual non-interference established."[14] Johnson then followed Indigenous protocols in sealing and certifying the agreement that had been reached – by giving tangible marks of it that could be regularly displayed as both proof and reminder of the promises made and the understanding reached.[15] He also followed a long-standing tradition in

our country of offering a number of wampum belts as these
tangible markers. These belts, also known as collars,[16] origin-
ated with the Haudenosaunee in their first dealings with
Europeans, including the British.[17] The Haudenosaunee also
used them in their first dealings with the Huron-Wendat,[18] and
the Huron-Wendat then used belts in their treating (or treaty
making) with us, the Nishnaabeg.

These belts were more than a public sign of a covenanted
agreement, however. They were also a record of what was
agreed to, with meaning encoded both in the symbols woven
into the belts and in the numbers of shell beads in a given
row or rows.[19] Successive generations of elders decoded these
meanings to retell the story of the treaty's commitments and
understandings.

Johnson called one of his belt gifts the "Belt of the Covenant Chain."[20] When the ends of the belt were drawn together
to form a collar, the beadwork at each end completed the image of two diamonds side by side.[21] The diamond represents a
nation, which is synonymous with a council fire. Having two
diamonds together conveys two nations in alliance;[22] here, the
British and the Western Confederacy.

The nature of the alliance, continuing its association
with the multinational Covenant Chain of Friendship,[23] was
depicted in the middle of the belt. There are two stylized
humans holding hands, with hearts (each slightly different)
worked into the beadwork at the centre of their chests. This
was to demonstrate Johnson's claim "that despite the distance
between his house (or mat) and the Anishinaabe's, his heart
was always close to theirs."[24]

A second wampum belt was the "Twenty-Four Nations
Belt." It depicted twenty-four stylized figures linked arm in
arm, with the Anishinaabek Nations drawing a British vessel
laden with presents from across the Atlantic and anchoring it
to North America – a token of the Crown's fiduciary commit-
ment to its treaty partners.

In the stories we grew up hearing, a two-row wampum belt
was also presented. Its two rows of purple quahog shells on a
bed of white whelk shells depicted a sailing ship and a canoe
travelling side by side down the river of life, with the three
shells connecting these two lines representing peace, respect,

and friendship. This belt with this image had been used by the Haudenosaunee from their earliest dealings with their British allies to signify and affirm autonomy, with the three connecting shells representing the principles that should guide relations between them. The belt had come to be widely understood as "a diplomatic convention that recognizes interaction and separation of settler and First Nation societies."[25] Its use at Niagara would be taken to signify that "the principles it represents were renewed in 1764."

Perhaps to bolster the English record of this understanding, William Johnson wrote to General Thomas Gage that same year, 1764: "You may be assured that none of the Six Nations or Western Indians ever declared themselves *subjects,* or will ever consider themselves in that light ... The very idea of subjection would fill them with horror."[26]

While the Niagara treaty's purpose was largely to lay a secure groundwork for ongoing trade, it also dealt with other important matters. One of these was to enshrine the notion of sharing the land, with any surrender of it for settlement to be negotiated by agents of the Crown only. This solved the problem of settlers squatting on our land.

But sharing the land for hunting and trapping and settling on it permanently were very different things, and the difference in meaning went deep. Tecumseh was a visionary leader who recognized this. As the British organized more and more treaty councils about more and more land for settlement, Tecumseh rallied the Anishinaabeg around the idea of creating a sovereign Anishinaabeg state/jurisdiction on land still protected as ours under the Royal Proclamation. He then mobilized a two-thousand–strong Anishinaabe fighting force including Shawnee, Potawatomi, Sauk, Winnebago, and Ota'wa warriors to fight on behalf of the British during the War of 1812.[27] The idea was that, when the British (with the help of the Nishnaabeg) prevailed over the Americans, they would back this plan.

The Anishinaabe fighting presence was seen as decisive in helping to repulse an American invasion.[28] But Tecumseh was killed during that decisive battle, at Moraviantown, and his plan was left unfulfilled.[29]

And the Loyalists and other settlers kept coming, following the "trail of the black walnut" as some of the newcomers put it, understanding the walnut tree to be a sign of good, deep soil for farming.[30] The more they came, the more colonization of our land began to change too, as Tecumseh had foreseen. Canadian historians call it a transition from a staples-extracting colony to a settler colony. The newcomers no longer wanted to just take furs and trees from our territories and go away again, back home to Europe. Now they wanted to stay on our land, settle on it and make it their home too.

Through the 1800s, successive superintendents of Indian Affairs called together more and more treaty councils to secure more and more land for settlement. The largest of these at the time was the Huron Tract Treaty, and it covered a big part of what is now southwestern Ontario, where we lived. Negotiations for this began in 1818.

According to one scholarly account, our people were told that they would be permitted to fish and hunt in their old locations as before.[31] Superintendent of Indian Affairs Thomas McKee told one treaty council meeting with thirteen Ojibway chiefs that the king "wanted this area 'not for his own use but for the use of his Indian children and you yourselves will be as welcome as any others to come and live therein.' ... [The Ojibway-Anishinaabe] were not aware that they were surrendering the land for white settlement."[32] Not then and not now either. Our ancestors agreed to share the land. We do not even have a word for surrender.

The treaty formally decreed that the land at Stoney Point and Kettle Point would remain exclusively ours: "For the exclusive use, benefit and enjoyment of the Nishnaabeg of Kettle Point and Stoney Point." For us, though, it was our place before the treaty, and that is what was important to us; not the treaty. The treaty was for the settlers, not us really. We just kept the lands that were the most important to us; the rest could be shared.

The original sketch of the land associated with the treaty also indicated that the land to be shared was around 712,000 acres, not the well over 2 million acres the colonial government ended up taking.[33] The larger amount was written down in the treaty document, along with the word "surrender," and although most of the chiefs "signed" it (using their clan symbol), most if not all were unable to read the English text where these numbers and the phrase "cede and surrender" were recorded. Still, our understanding, which has been handed down to us from our elders, recorded in their memories, is that this land was to be shared. Like in the two-row wampum belt with those two boats travelling side by side; you got your boat, we got our boat. That is the way it's meant to be.

Our Nishnaabe forebears carried on with their lives, unaware of how much change had been set in motion. They continued their seasonal movements through their vast territory, "coming together for the spring and fall fisheries, travelling in smaller groups to their more remote hunting grounds for the winter, and moving to the maple sugar camps before congregating again at their fishing sites."[34] They also always took time to visit their ancestral burial grounds, to feed the spirits. Anishinaabe legal historian Darlene Johnston documented the importance of these visits for the Ipperwash Inquiry:

"For the Anishnaabeg," she wrote, "the Great Lakes Region is more than geography. It is a spiritual landscape formed by and embedded with the regenerative potential of the First Ones who gave it form and to whom they owe their existence."[35]

The mark made by our Aazhoodena/Stoney Point Chippewa chief, Waapagance,[36] when signing the draft Huron Tract Treaty is a key to this. He "signed" with a pictograph, a stylized drawing of a caribou. This designated his *dodem,* or "clan totem," and, through it, the particular place from which his ancestors had emerged and to which, therefore, he and his clan belonged. In the Anishinaabe Creation story, which is a post-flood re-creation story, humans owe their existence to animals.

In her research paper, Darlene Johnston draws on an account of this recorded by Nicholas Perrot, one of the first French officials to overwinter in the area, deferring to this recording of the original story because, as she wrote, "I lack the authority and fluency required to present the oral tradition" herself.[37] In an English translation of Perrot's version of what he was

told, the story begins after the flood when the land animals
are surviving on a great wooden raft. Their leader, the Great
Hare, Michabous, knows they need land to survive and that it
is still there, buried under all the water. On behalf of all the
animals, he asks Beaver to dive down in search of some soil
from which they can regenerate land on which to live.[38] When
Beaver resurfaces, nearly dead, he has found nothing. Otter
tries next, and he too comes back to the surface with nothing.
Then the smallest of the animals, the muskrat, dives down
into the deep. He is gone for nearly twenty-four hours and
when Muskrat resurfaces, he is motionless and belly up, but
all four of his paws are clenched. The other animals carefully
pull him onto the raft and one by one unclench his paws. In
the fourth one they search, they find a single grain of sand.
The Great Hare drops this onto the surface of the raft and
immediately it begins to increase.

According to the story, he took this and scattered it about,
and it kept increasing. Soon it had formed itself into a moun-
tain, and so the Great Hare started to walk around it, creating
a path and more land. He sent the Fox out to explore the land,
giving him the same power to extend it further. And so the
Anishinaabeg world of the Great Lakes came into being –
created, Johnston notes, "for mutual sustenance, not personal
gain" and through acts of "cooperation and bravery," with the
Great Hare's leadership based on "persuasion, not coercion."[39]
At its centre, the raft became an island, called Michilimakinac,
situated in the present-day strait between Lake Huron and
Lake Michigan.

After this landscape was recreated, all the animals, the First
Ones, took up residence in whatever part of it best suited their
needs. Johnston continues, from Perrot's memoirs:

> When the first ones died, the Great Hare caused the birth
> of men from their corpses, as also from those of the fishes
> that were found along the shores of the rivers which he had
> formed in creating the land. Accordingly, some of the [people]
> derive their origins from a bear, others from a moose ... You
> will hear them say that their villages each bear the name of
> the animal which has given its people their being.[40]

"Totems were the glue that held the Anishnabeg Great Lakes world together,"[41] Johnston has written. They tied particular groups of families together in one place of origin and reminded them to honour it as an enduringly spiritual space. As one result of this, it was important for people to be buried in their particular homeland. "The permanence of the connection between body and soul was grounded in a particular landscape."[42] It was equally important to keep that connection alive by visiting the dead and putting down tobacco, food, and other gifts to honour them.

> In Anishnabeg culture, there is an ongoing relationship between the Dead and the Living; between ancestors and descendants. It is the obligation of the Living to ensure that their relatives are buried in the proper manner and in the proper place and to protect them from disturbance or desecration. Failure to perform this duty harms not only the Dead but also the Living. The dead need to be sheltered and fed, to be visited and feasted. These traditions continue to exhibit powerful continuity.[43]

The Jesuit Chronicles show that some of the first European newcomers understood this, or tried to, it seems. Father Jean de Brébeuf recorded his understanding of what he was told:

> many believe we have two souls ... the one separates itself from the body at death, yet remains in the Cemetery until the feast of the Dead ... The other is, as it were, bound to the body and informs, so to speak, the corpse; it remains in the grave of the dead after the feast and never leaves it ... It shows why they call the bones of the dead *Atisken,* "the souls."[44]

The people many of us are descended from would have kept this up as much as they could, visiting the burial grounds to keep the connection going. But the settlers kept coming. By as early as 1830, their demands for our land and their habit of squatting on it regardless of the rules were threatening that sacred connection. The lieutenant governor of Upper Canada, Sir John Colborne, offered housing and education assistance to those nations who would gather more compactly into villages.

He sent instructions about this to the superintendent of Indian Affairs for the region at the time, George Ironside. He told Ironside to switch the annual treaty gifts from fishing and hunting supplies to gifts of farming equipment instead, to curb "the wandering habits" of the Anishinaabeg. He added: "And he will impress upon them the necessity of the change proposed in their present habits and customs ... and that they ought to lose no time in clearing and cultivating their own lands, and making themselves as independent as the settlers are, who gradually close around them, and will soon occupy their hunting grounds."[45] He hoped that, combined with the building of schools and some houses on reserves, this might happen.

He didn't see that our people, the Nishnaabeg, were continuing to be independent, but in our own way. We adopted things the newcomers brought, but into our way of life. Our forebears started to use European tools in hunting and trapping; they also learned from their earliest relations with the settler-farmers. Those relations were often reciprocal. In fact, the first settlers depended a lot on their Nishnaabe neighbours, not just for guiding, help in hunting and in killing marauding bears, but for day to day survival. Some settler stories make reference to Indian corn as among their first crops. They also learned how to make maple syrup and tan hides, and how to use our herbal medicines.[46] When the Huron Tract Treaty was being negotiated in the 1820s, the Nishnaabeg had requested the services of a blacksmith and someone knowledgeable about raising cows and horses.[47] This tells us that they were starting to acquire horses and cows even then.[48] They were not just hunters and gatherers; they were hunter-gatherers and starting to be farmers too.

THE INDIAN ACT

Confederation went ahead with no Nishnaabeg or other Indigenous Nations at the talks to help create and shape it. After Confederation happened, the British government turned over its responsibility for Indigenous affairs in the former British colonies to Canada. The record of what happened next is pretty clear. We Nishnaabeg became "the

Indian problem," the subject of three government commissions.[49] We had no voice, no role in any of these either. In 1876, the Canadian Parliament passed the Indian Act. Among the many ways in which this act tried to take over and control our lives, it imposed a popular-vote form of government on top of and taking precedence over our traditional self-governance, with decisions by consensus and inherited leadership responsibilities. This new government took the form of band councils. Their authority was limited, and voting was restricted to men only. The act redefined us as "wards" of the state, not members of our own clans and nations. And it defined a person as "an individual other than an Indian."[50]

Nothing had changed since the 1857 Act to Encourage the Gradual Civilization of the Indian Tribes. This colonial law set out various ways in which Nishnaabeg as individuals could essentially graduate out of their own clans and nations and become "enfranchised" as "civilized" Canadian citizens. Still, doing this was voluntary, and apparently only one person applied.[51] The Indian Act went further. It introduced involuntary enfranchisement for people who got a university education, joined the army, or spent any length of time living off the reserve. The government also set up forced assimilation centres called residential schools for our children,[52] deliberately remote from our reserves to cut them off from home. In 1920, an amendment to the act made residential school attendance compulsory.

This was devastating. Families lost their children as sons and daughters from ages as young as five to at least sixteen were forcibly taken away. Families were allowed visits only by special permission, and the children were only allowed to go home on designated holidays. The children lost everything: not just their parents and extended families, not just the familiar sights, sounds, and smells of home and being on the land of their home reserve, but also their language and the fluent continuity, from one generation to the next, of traditions and life skills – all the teachings and ceremonies, all the practices and protocols that help us sustain our Nishnaabe way of life on the land and the world view guiding it. Instead, the boys learned farm chores, milking up to forty cows morning and night. They were also sent out on road construction and ditch-digging crews. The girls worked in the gardens and kitchen and at the sewing machines, with some of them sent out to the homes of the local well-to-do to sew for them.

Bonnie Bressette's mother, Hilda, was kept back during summer holidays to sew school uniforms for the coming year. Bonnie carries the memory and the pain of it still. "My mum didn't have no English language when she went there. She only spoke Nishinaabe language, and they were beaten whenever they spoke the language. One time, she was sewing. They had these big sewing machines, and she was sewing this thick material and the needle went right through her thumb – and she forgot her English and started yelling for help in the language, and the headmistress that was there told her she was not going to help her 'til she spoke in English, and my mum said that was the hardest thing when she was hurting, to remember English to ask for help ...

"The only time I heard my mother speak the language was maybe when she was with some of the [other] people that still had their language. I was fifty years old when she apologized to me for not giving me all the teachings as a Nishnaabe-kwe; an Aboriginal woman."

Marcia remembers her mother, Melva, crying when she talked about seeing her little brother Calvin being punished for speaking the language. "She remembered them knocking him right onto the floor, right off his chair when he spoke in our language."

Her father, Daniel, was not sent away to residential school. He attended the elementary school they still had on the reserve. So did Clifford George, though his sisters were taken. Sometimes the children would be kept hidden in the bush when the Indian agent or the Royal Canadian Mounted Police (RCMP) came looking for children in the fall, even though this was against the law. Bruce George was another who escaped residential school this way, attending the one-room school on the reserve. But like many of the boys, he was often needed to go cutting wood in the bush – not just for the family but to sell as firewood off the reserve.

The Indian Act gave the Indian agent more and more power. He had the authority to give or withhold a permit for anyone wanting to sell produce off the reserve. He was allowed to summarily convict people if they did not send their children to residential school, fining them two dollars or sending them to jail for ten days. He had the right to review and approve the agenda for band council meetings. He also attended all the meetings and made sure that no resolution was acted upon until it was approved by Indian Affairs.

Bonnie remembers because her father was active in the community, especially in organizing baseball games, and also served as a band councillor. "You couldn't do anything without the Indian agent. And if he didn't like what was going on, he just closed the books and closed the meeting ... When you had to live under Indian Affairs, that's the way life was."

We started losing some of our land too, at first just for road construction, such as replacing what had been a wagon trail through the reserve with what became Highway 21. The government then began treating this as the new border of the reserve. After World War I, there was mounting pressure for us to surrender the beautiful stretch of sandy beach and dunes that ran from Kettle Point to Stoney Point for summer cottages.

From what we know of what happened, a Sarnia land developer approached the Indian agent in 1927 with a view to buying a stretch of this beachfront property closest to Sarnia, in the Kettle Point Reserve. Money was offered to help make this go the way these men wanted – what the developer called signing bonuses and our leaders saw as bribes. The chief at the time, John Milliken, and two others, Sam Bressette and Robert George – grandfather to many involved in the actions in the 1990s – wrote to Indian Affairs when the Indian agent ignored their request to hold a council meeting to discuss the prospective sale. The record does not show whether permission to hold the meeting was ever given. But a vote was held, "bonus" money was paid, and the land surrender went ahead.

Indian Affairs did look into the matter. They decided that the vote had been legitimate and satisfied the requirements of the Indian Act. But the people here never accepted this, and in 1992 the Kettle and Stony Point First Nation took legal action, all the way to the Supreme Court. All the courts decided against the Nishnaabeg. Still, at the 1995 hearing by the Ontario Superior Court, Justice Killeen noted that "There can be little doubt that these cash payments, and the promises which preceded them, have an odour of moral failure about them."[53]

Meanwhile, in 1928, another Sarnia real estate developer (and future mayor of Sarnia) had approached Indian Affairs with a view to buying the beachfront associated with Stoney Point – 377 acres. He got support from the local Indian agent and the local member of Parliament too. The project seemed to move ahead quickly. A majority of the band members (men) voted to support the surrender, accepting the thirty-five dollars an acre the developer was offering the band. (Some historical research done by research consultant Joan Holmes for the Ipperwash Inquiry sheds light on the pressure they might have been under. It explained that bands were often "desperate for capital for some kind of project ... because, as an Indian Band, they can't borrow money or get money in the way that any other Canadian citizen can."[54])

Less than ten years later, in 1936, these same Sarnia developers sold 109 of the 377 acres to the provincial government – for nearly one hundred dollars an acre – to create a provincial park called Ipperwash. The land included some burial grounds, though the government only officially acknowledged this fact in 1950 when some graves were desecrated by a bulldozer while a reservoir was being excavated in the park. A report on this was filed with the provincial government, and that's all that happened.

One of the names associated with that Stoney Point land turned into the park was Albert George, known to us as Kamaanii. He was the great-grandfather of Dudley George – and others of us too, including Marcia Simon, Glenn George, Bonnie Bressette, and of course, Cully and Pierre, Dudley's sister and brother. We knew that Kamaanii's homestead was there, and he might have been buried there too. Plus, the Kettle and Stony Point band council passed a resolution (on August 12, 1937) asking the provincial government to fence off the burial grounds so they could be protected as sacred ground. The Indian agent approved the resolution and passed it on to his superiors at the Department of Indian Affairs. The secretary of the Indian Affairs Branch duly wrote to the Ontario deputy minister of the Department of Lands and Forests, which was responsible for provincial parks, relaying this request. The deputy minister in turn promised to "do my best to respect the natural wishes of the Indians" and to see what he could do.[55]

Life on the reserve continued, with its seasonal rituals, its familiar routines of fishing and hunting, planting and harvesting, canning fruit and storing vegetables in the root house, plus mending things like fishing nets and making things like baskets, axe handles, and furniture. Each activity produced its familiar sounds, though one persisted from season to season: the steady thonk of an axe-head against a felled log of black ash, sometimes accompanied by someone singing something slow and steady that got everyone pounding to the same rhythm. Thonk, thonk, thonk, up and down the length of the log, loosening the fibres inside, separating the spring wood from the summer wood so the annual growth rings could be peeled off one by one, with each strip then split into thinner and thinner splints.[56] These were then woven into baskets of various sizes and even sunhats for local cottagers.

Marcia Simon and Bonnie Bressette's Grandma Flora used to make
and sell these. Nearly a century later, one of Bonnie's granddaughters
would use one of these exquisitely crafted hats as the basis of her
master's thesis on Indigenous educational policy and leadership.
Bonnie had noticed the hat in one of the cottages she used to clean
and arranged to acquire it from the person who had purchased it from
Flora.

A softer sound but just as prevalent came from the wooden work-
benches; the hand-hewn wooden foot pedal clunking down to hold a
length of hickory being fashioned into an axe handle or some maple,
birch, or cedar being chiselled and planed (using a draw knife) into
the leg of a table or chair. From a first recorded sale, presumably to
a settler, in 1834, the Nishnaabeg of Stoney Point built up a modest
local craft-selling business.

Marcia: "We were really known for our cedar furniture."

Whatever cash needs this and the traplines did not supply our
people earned as hired hands working for local farmers, tossing hay
onto wagons and into haylofts, stooking grain and gathering up the
sheaves for threshing and, by the 1920s and '30s, working in the
fields at the new market gardens.

Clifford George was among those who walked four or five kilometres each way to work at the Celery Gardens (we called it "The
Bog"), "lifting up the celery ... and an awful lot of onions and stuff
like that," for $1.25 a day.

But life was still rooted, deeply, on the reserve. The land sustained
us in our daily lives and all this meant to us, and we expected this to
continue.

Clifford: "We had everything good here; good relationships, good
relationship with the next reserve ... We were very poor, but we managed. We were self-sufficient here, self-supporting completely."

CHAPTER TWO

"The House Was Gone"

I n February 1942, the federal government decided to take over our whole reserve and turn it into an army training camp called Camp Ipperwash. They decided to do this to avoid the cost of installing a water pipe from Lake Huron to an existing army base farther inland. They reasoned too that they could take the land because in their eyes it was undeveloped and unproductive. Some of the documentation that came to light during the Ipperwash Inquiry used these words. The Indian agent of the day reported that the site was also ideally suited as a training ground, "with the open lake as a background for rifle ranges." As well, he wrote: "Personally, I think this is a wonderful opportunity to gather a few straggling Indians and locate them permanently with the main body of the band at Kettle Point. It would solve many problems and dispense with a great deal of expense ... such as schools, roads, visitations, etc."

Although four separate reserves were created through the 1827 Huron Tract Treaty, each with its own history and often different traditions and even slight differences in dialect, the colonial authorities decided to treat them all as one "band" for administrative convenience. Walpole Island was the first to be given its own band status, in 1836, followed by the Sarnia reserve in 1919. But instead of giving Kettle Point and Stoney Point each our own band status, too, which would have made sense and been more convenient for us, the government kept us administratively tied together. It was a set-up for trouble, a divide-and-rule kind of trouble, some of us thought. Because by then the government had imposed its own popular-vote type of self-government on the reserves, which meant a single elected band council for both Kettle Point and Stoney Point. We, those "few straggling Indians" at Stoney Point, were somewhere between eighteen and twenty-two families, although Indian Affairs had it down as fourteen in their records. Either way, there were just over seventy people living in Stoney Point, compared to at least double that number at Kettle Point.

We Stoney Pointers – or, rather, our parents and grandparents – learned of the government's takeover plan through a notice the Indian agent posted outside our church. It was a Methodist church with a Native man preaching inside at the time.

Rose: "I remember everybody thought they were very disrespectful to come in and do this while they were having a service."

Suddenly too there were strangers on our land, going around drilling holes for some reason.

Janet: "I believe it was 1938 that they went on my mother's property. And it was under Chief Frank Bressette at the time. He didn't even ask my grandmother to go, that the ministry wanted to drill on her land. So there was bad feelings there.

"And she did ask them: What are yous doing on my property? He dismissed her! Maybe because she couldn't speak English." She never did find out why they were drilling. None of us did.

Next thing we knew, the Indian agent was following through on instructions to remove any "white" people living at Kettle Point. "White" meant any of the local Nishnaabe-kwe (women) who had brought non-Native men home to marry. When they did this, they lost their official "status" as Indians under the Indian Act. In the eyes of the government, these Nishnaabe-kwe became officially "white."

In March 1942, some of our parents and grandparents sent a letter to the government in Ottawa, reminding them of George III's Royal Proclamation and the Huron Tract Treaty's promise that Stoney Point was reserved for our "exclusive use and enjoyment" for all time. "So please accept this as our final answer of not wishing to sell or leave the Stoney Point Reservation," they wrote. This was followed, on March 25, by a petition from the Kettle Point and Stoney Point War Workers Organization recalling the memory of ancestors who had fought as allies to the British in the War of 1812 under Tecumseh. They also reminded the government that the Nishnaabeg were working and fighting as allies once again – not just in local armament industries but also as enlisted soldiers. Men like Clifford George were already overseas at the time. "What will our boys think who have signed up for active service ..." they asked, "when they find no home and land to fall back on when they return home after the war?"

On April 1, the Indian agent arranged to hold a surrender vote, with funds specially allocated to bus in people no longer living on the reserve who might bolster the vote for yes. Fifty-nine of the seventy-two eligible voters voted no. No surrender. Two weeks later, the government issued Privy Council Order #2913, authorizing the appropriation of the reserve under the War Measures Act. It also allocated fifty thousand dollars to cover the cost of removing the Indians plus "their buildings, chattels" off the reserve. Most of that money was channelled through the Indian agent, M.W. McCracken, directly to the movers and local building-materials suppliers. In an October 8, 1942, memo to his superiors, McCracken wrote that "In my opinion, this procedure is more desirable than giving thim [*sic*] the money in their own hands which in many cases would be squandered on an old motor car or other similar expenditure."

And then the army came. There were big dump trucks and bulldozers and other equipment. They started clearing our land. They started drilling and digging too, excavating a whole quarry where Rose Elijah (later, Manning)'s family were still living. They crushed up that stone and used it to lay down roads all through our bush. And Ollie Tremain, a local trucker, also came.

Suddenly five-year old Bonnie's home was being lifted into the air and plunked down onto the flat back of his truck. "Why is our house up there?" she asked her father.

"He said we had to move away because there was a war on and that after the war we'd be moving back."

Bonnie has a black-and-white photo of her and her sister, Laura ("Fidgie"), wearing pretty smock-fronted dresses. It was taken that day, possibly by her mother, the dresses a product of their mother's fine sewing.

"Why did we have to get all dressed up for that hurtful day? It wasn't 'til later on, talking with our older women that I could understand: 'You might be doing this to us, but we still have our pride and our dignity.'"

Rose: "Some were moved forcefully. Some were moved while they were at work. They jacked up their house and took it without even their wrapping their dishes up, and they came home with broken dishes on the floor and no handles on their cups. There was a lot of stories like that. There was one person, she put herself in front of Mr. Tremain's truck because she didn't want to move." Her parents had enough advance warning that they took Rose away that day.

"I woke up in this big swamp with our house just on boulders, and when you tried to go outside, there was nothing but reeds and weeds."

There was no predicting when our homes were going to be moved because Mr. Tremain, who had been given the contract to do the work, apparently took on another job at the same time. He moved our homes when he could fit us into his schedule.

Janet: "Mum and Dad knew they were going to be moved, but they didn't know when. One day after work, Mum came home and found no house. The house was gone. It was devastating for her; they were never given notice.

"Mum and Dad went up to Kettle Point to find their home sitting on four big stones – in a swamp. And all their possessions were in disarray; dishes broken. They were just dishes, but they meant a lot to her. They were probably her grandmother's dishes or her grandpa's. Things that she treasured.

"So Mum had to start all over again, and Dad, to make a home in that area. I don't know how Mum lived through it. She did; they were strong, strong people. I had twin sisters born just after that; they died, and I blame that water ...

"We were all affected. It still does affect us today – that move in 1942."

Like Janet's mum, Pearl George, Bonnie's parents, Bruce and Hilda, had family property in Kettle Point to which they could relocate their Stoney Point home.[1] This was Hilda's family home, Bonnie's Grandma Flora's place. Bonnie remembers her family's little bungalow sitting in an empty field there, grasses and weeds growing all around it higher than Bonnie's waist. It was perched on timber logs and stayed that way until Bonnie's father could get together the money to pour a proper foundation. The Indian agent provided no help.

A couple of months later, Bruce and his good friend Sheldon Cloud went back to Stoney Point thinking there would be food to harvest from their gardens.

"Those guys just stood and stared. They went to the next place and the next. All the gardens were flattened. Everything they counted on, and the army ploughed all them gardens under with some great big machine. Everything they counted on to live. If you didn't have a garden, you couldn't live in the winter."

The family was lucky; they had Grandma Flora's home and her garden to fall back on. The contents of her root house kept them alive that first winter.

Our parents and grandparents from Stoney Point didn't just lose their gardens and fruit trees. Everything – their barns and sheds, root cellars and water wells – was bulldozed and destroyed by the army. Some of us are still wondering where the horses, cows, geese, and other animals went. Rumour had it that the men building the army base simply slaughtered them and used them as food for themselves. There seems to be no record of this on file, no accounting of all the animals. They simply disappeared.

The archives do contain a letter the government received on September 14, 1942, signed by Mrs. Robert George. "You don't know how it feels to be ordered out," she wrote, "losing our beloved ground for a few dollars,[2] and our belongings dumped into a small plot of ground, no land for our children and our children's babies." And cut off from family in the burial grounds too.

Rose: "It's sad to leave your grandfather and sister behind there. And the army promised us that they would look after the graveyard, and they would take good care of it, but they never did. It was shot all to pieces, and there was no regard for the people that was buried there. I guess they just thought, 'Well, they're dead and they don't know anything. They're just Natives.'"

Bonnie: "There was people at Kettle Point too. The Indian agent didn't even ask if they can move somebody's house on there at Kettle Point. They just went and moved it on that land and never even asked that family if they could."

The newcomers were called "refugees" and worse. The children were bullied at school.

Janet: "The Nishnaabeg of Aazhoodena, they were heartbroken and didn't want to live at Kettle Point. Kettle Pointers didn't want Stoney Pointers either. The men from Stoney Point no longer participated in elections because they were not from here. Kettle Point men made all the decisions. This went on for many years."

A 1998 master's thesis cited by one of the researchers for the Ipperwash Inquiry noted:

The change from forty acre parcels to two acres severely impeded farming efforts, particularly on the swampland on the 14th Concession. Removal onto new land in the midst of the growing season prevented the families from growing needed winter food. In addition, the distance from the established clientele for the[ir] craft industry, and from local farmers who were employers, reduced the opportunity to make money. Within the first year of removal, many families were forced onto welfare or off-Reserve in order to survive.[3]

"They was starving," Clifford George told the Ipperwash Inquiry. "That's how come my father [Bill George] ended up working in the Forest Basket Company. Employment was coming up a little bit [with the war on] but it was very difficult for some of them people [without a car] because that fourteen-mile round trip made the whole difference.

"It was very difficult for some of them. Some of them old people that never drank in their life started drinking ... you know, just to relieve all the problems they were facing ... A lot of old people passed away on account of that ... Their own lands, which they called their own lands, to be moved [away] and then, not wanted where they are ... The government just doesn't realize, you know, the feelings of some of these people."

CHAPTER THREE

Disruption and Determination

Clifford George was earning his first medal fighting overseas in World War II when his family was forced out of their home at Stoney Point. He spent the last three months of the war in a prisoner-of-war camp in northern Italy, severely malnourished from the minimal food available.

His mother had died shortly after he went overseas and was buried on the reserve; the burial grounds are on a sandy hillside not far from the lake.

"There was a white picket fence around there, about halfway down, and that's where all the dignitaries were buried, like clan mothers and chiefs and stuff like that ... and us kids weren't allowed to go in there.

"I remember my father writing to me [overseas]. 'Don't worry about our cemetery. It's well looked after' ... It's in the books that they, the army that took over, they would look after it."

Clifford was reminded of this when he was part of retaking the French village of Dieppe, "and I saw all the crosses, the well-kept crosses ... We were amazed at that, to see how well they looked after our ... Canadian crosses."

When he was well enough to be sent home, he went to the Ipperwash army base and asked permission to visit his mother's grave. Permission, too, for his two brothers who had also served overseas; one (Ken) was still suffering from shell shock.

"So we went there, and it was absolute devastation."

He and his brothers stood there stunned "to see the mess that the [burial grounds] was. We couldn't even tell where my mother was buried ... There was a headstone and it was all pockmarked with rifles. It was a mess, because they even fired at it with their rifles – and there was bandoliers of shells just over the posts and stuff like that there; blanks of course, where they were playing soldier.

"We were crying our eyes out. Good hardened soldiers crying. I told the people there, you know, that's a shame, what you've done. We only had just a rough idea where my mother was buried."

He got a job as custodian at the base, looking after the army's property, taking things to the dump near the back of the base, hearing talk about a canister of nerve gas having been rolled into one of the bayous. That's what we call the string of little inland lakes that run along the inside of the dunes of the shoreline of Lake Huron.

He wanted to build a home for himself and the war bride he had brought home with him from England, and he wanted to do this at Kettle Point. For that, though, he needed an allotment of land there because he could not get what he should have been entitled to at Stoney Point. He approached the Indian agent, who was in charge of this and who lived in Sarnia.

"I hitchhiked there, and I told him that I want a piece of land to build a home on, because at that time there was a little money available." (Returning Native vets received $2,200 to help them build a home, et cetera. Non-Native soldiers, he learned later, got more than double that – $5,500.[1])

"The Indian agent, he swore, he definitely swore at me. He said you're not bringing that White woman to this godforsaken reserve, which will never see hydro, will never see phones, will never see inside plumbing. No sir, you're not going to get no land ... He put an awful guilt trip on me ...

"And then, I don't know whether he called me Mr. George or Clifford. I don't remember. But he said, 'Just wait a minute. I'll tell you what I'll do. I'll get you some money for a down payment on a house in Forest where you belong' ...

"So, anyway, about a month later I had a notice to come and – come and get your cheque. So I got one of my friends to drive me to Sarnia where his office was and they hand me an envelope – a big four hundred dollars for a down payment on a house. And then about a month later, I got this special letter from Ottawa and inside it was a blue card and they said I can use this anywhere. You are now a white man."

Clifford had been involuntarily "enfranchised" (in other words, he had lost his status) under the Indian Act.[2]

"It disentitled me completely" from being able to live on the reserve, he told Justice Linden at the Ipperwash Inquiry. And he had not known.

"I was absolutely unaware of what they done to me. I sold my rights as an Indian and I didn't know it."[3]

He raised his family first in Forest and then in Sarnia. But he always went back, and when he heard about some prayer meetings at Daniel and Melva George's home at Kettle Point, he started to attend.

Rose Manning's home was one of the last to be moved. She remembered the quarry filling up with water and wanting to go swimming and her mother being afraid that she might drown.

Later, "I went back with my grandmother, Lena, who used to go back there picking her medicines or her berries or bittersweet. She didn't want to go alone and I just went with her. I remember playing around and picking berries and eating them. And then when they would start shooting, she'd say, let's get out of here."

She had attended the day school at Stoney Point and continued on at the one in Kettle Point. Then she married an Irish Canadian, Murray Alfred Manning, and moved to his family farm outside Watford, near Sarnia. She lost her status as an official Indian but raised her twelve children on stovetop bannock, which she called *bkwezhgan* (our word for "bread"), and sent them back to Stoney when she could.

"One of my daughters worked as a salad girl [in the army base kitchen during the summer]. And then one of my granddaughters too. I had three or four boys that went in there too, as cadets, and they were always in that bush there. And they would feed all those cadets and buy shoes for them. So I put as many as I could in for cadets. Just my boys."

Daniel George also grew up at Stoney Point. He was almost twenty-one and he would have been entitled to forty acres of his own where he could start a family when the government takeover cut him off. He was forced off the land that had sustained the family for so many generations. After the war, he made a living as a bulldozer operator, landscaping the hills of a park in Sarnia, going all over, wherever there was work.

Marcia: "He went to Munsee and Chippewas on the Thames and the Six Nations [reserve] – and those others, the [highways] 401 and the 402 when they put those in. He knew how to operate all that other equipment too: the paver with those big rollers, and the grader, and the dump trucks; he could drive all those things.

"And he shared that with the young men – his sons, and when he was working over at Chippewas of the Thames, he taught all those young men there how to use that equipment, and they used to visit him; they looked up to him."

Around here, a lot of people called him the Dozer Man because he used his machine to help out, even clearing snow from people's back lanes and driveways, keeping alive our understanding of work. In our language, the word for "work" is *anookiiwin,* which is more like a responsibility than a job, and is closely tied to our ideas of "duty" and "right." So work is not just for ourselves but part of our duty to support our family and community.[4]

But Daniel also worked moving debris in the fibreglass dump, all in an unenclosed cab; after years of inhaling dust, he developed emphysema.

He was also a carpenter. Once he broke his ankle. But he had to keep going, so he cut and whittled a peg leg for himself. And it worked. Like others of that generation who kept Stoney Point alive in their memory, he also found ways to sneak in and move around our former territory, often unnoticed by the military police on patrol. He ran a trapline there for years. He also kept an eye out for the red flag. That signalled action at the ranges: rifles being shot, grenade launchers, mortar shells. On days when the red flag was down, he sometimes brought his wife, Melva, and his children, including Marcia and Glenn.

Marcia remembers: "There was a little lake there by the highway [the former quarry on the Elijah homestead]. Stone Crusher they called it, and we would go in there and skate ... There were other times when we would go down what's now called the Army Camp Road as far as the turnoff toward the burial grounds. And right near there, there's also the dump, and we would go and rummage through there for any treasures we could find and take them home – pop bottles. We would wash them up and sell them. .

"We would go and visit the burial grounds, and we have a story that we joke about. At one point there was a fence up, and it was labelled 'out of bounds' and my sister, she was just learning to read, and she said it was 'out of bones.'"

Glenn also remembers those days: "We used to go get stuff out of the dump, like nails. We used to have to pick them up and take them

home and straighten them out because we were going to use them to
build a shed ...

"We used to always take our rides down to the lakefront there.
Every time we drove by, like, it was 'there's where my house used to
be' ... It was a constant thing."

Marcia: "As part of his story that this is our homeland, my dad
would take us there ... The top of the well was still there – the rocks
and the bricks ... So we grew up knowing it was ours. And we were
always told that they took it over but their *promise* was that it would
be returned at the end of the war. We had this *ingrained* into us.

"He was my inspiration to do all that I did."

Glenn: "As a young kid, I was always the guy they sent in, sent in
to the band office [in Kettle Point] to go get the woodcutting permit
... It was just, like, when you want to go gather something, it was
always put to my parents you had to go and ask somebody. You had
to go to the band office and ask somebody to go on your land because
... it was taken away."

Once a year, the army allowed former Stoney Point residents to
cut firewood inside the army camp; permits were issued through the
band office. "And my dad and my uncle Abe and my cousins, we used
to have tractors and old trucks with trailers, and you had to get it
done – in two days, to burn all year ...

"And some of my nephews and that, seeing how hard it was; they
used to look at us as kind of like little slaves or whatever, but we
didn't look at it like that; it was a social gathering for us, to go in the
bush and, you know, you had tea ...

"Even if there was fences like there are today, it doesn't stop people
from entering there and gathering whatever they needed to gather,
whether it be food or medicines or whatever ... Even though our people
weren't living there ... there was always people that went in there to
gather those foods.

"It's like one of those things that you might be able to take away
the land, but you're not going to take away the medicines ... Like, the
way of life that we were brought up [to] is that we had to gather these
things. It's one of those things that you're comfortable with ...

"Sometimes it's just where some people want to go, you know;
offer tobacco or visit, even just to go and look at the old [burial]
grounds ...

"My mother was taken away and put in residential school. And, I
think she protected me to that part where she didn't tell me what

went on ... I don't think it's as bad as what happened to my dad ... liv[ing] with the fear, you know, having the might of an army coming in to move you off your land. My dad was twenty-one years old when this happened. And, you know, that's a part of me ...

"And there's a thing that my dad used to always say, if he was having a drink or something. He would always almost be in tears about not having any inheritance for his boys."

Daniel and Melva's grandson Kevin recalls: "Some of my earliest memories are of Stoney Point. My grandfather was in there cutting wood with his buddy, like in a work bee. I was probably three years old, sittin' in the back of the truck watchin' them guys cutting wood. And they'd shut everything off and told me to be quiet when the range patrol come by. Don't ask me how you can keep quiet cutting wood, but they managed to do it. I remember one story. My grandfather, he liked his whisky, eh? And he was stopped by a teenage army brat and told he wasn't allowed to do that. And my grandfather, I guess he'd had enough and was, what you say *giiwshkwebii* in our language – a little wobbly with the drink, and he decided to let loose and give that youngster a piece of his mind. Apparently the army guy was crying and let them go when everything was done and said. You know? When you're right, you're right.

"I was raised by them to be proud of who I am, where I come from and never to forget that.

"I got into trouble at school once on account of that. I got put out of class for arguing with the teacher about the Potawatomis being extinct – knowing full well that we aren't. My grandfather and grandmother were one of the ones that fought to have the Potawatomis in Canada recognized."

Daniel's brother Abraham (Abe) also got emphysema because he too drove a bulldozer without a cab. His daughter Joy (Lewis) remembers him growing up. "He was a jack-of-all-trades. He could do everything: carpenter, mechanic, operating machinery, bulldozer. He was in the bush all the time too, cutting wood, trapping. Selling fur."

She also remembers having to grow up in Kettle Point. "Even though I'm half and half – half Stoney Point and [through her mother] half Kettle Point, I was picked on; teased and bullied and pushed around. I remember my brother Stewart ["Worm"], he was a teenager, and he was at the pow wow down at Kettle Point, and he got jumped on by the Bressettes. There was always this Bressette and George thing; that was right up until – well, even now. Their dad, Frank Bressette, he was chief back then ... I don't know why they resented us moving onto Kettle Point because we had to buy ugly old land and we had to buy soil to fill it in; fill in the swamp."

Another brother, Reginald (Reg), was the father of Anthony O'Brien ("Dudley") George, Perry (Pierre) George, and Carolyn (Cully) George. Like them, he was born and raised on the Stoney Point Reserve.

Pierre: "I think my dad was fifteen when they moved their house off the land there. They moved it right to Kettle Point."

Cully: "Maybe I was asking a lot of questions and stuff, but he told me a lot about when he lived there. About how they used to go cut wood, and he'd have to take the horses out to haul the wood back in. He told me about how deep the snow used to be back then ... and he told me about going with my grandparents to the market to take things that they had made to sell. My grandfather used to make axe handles and other woodwork things, and my grandmother made baskets and lace and quilts. They had gardens and stuff, but I don't think they ever took their produce there.

"And he might say how they had to move away when the war came along. And my dad was told that they would be able to go home after the war. He said he joined up [with] the army so that he could help get the war over, so he'd be *able* to move home."

That was understood to be the deal, at least by us. That's what they *told* us: we'd get to go home, we'd get our life back after the war was over. In May of 1946, the Indian Affairs Branch of the Department of Mines and Resources sent a letter to the deputy minister of National Defence (DND) to begin negotiations for the return of the land. And these started. But they broke off two years later. The military decided to turn Ipperwash into a cadet training camp; they would be keeping the land. Turns out, that order-in-council the federal government used to appropriate our reserve back in 1942 contained an extra phrase. "If, subsequent to the termination of the war, *the property was not required* by the Department of National Defence" it would be returned.[5] In their correspondence of the day, DND officials even acknowledged that this might be unjust and even a violation of the 1827 treaty. But they wanted to hang on to our land anyway. Camp Ipperwash would continue to exist, and Stoney Point/Aazhoodena would continue to not exist. Its existence would continue to be denied.

By then, Reginald (Reg) had married a woman from the Sarnia reserve, Genevieve, known as Jenny. She had gone straight from residential school into the army – the first Nishnaabe-kwe to serve. They had ten children.

Cully never knew her mother went to residential school. "She never talked about it. Still, I think it explains a lot of things about how she was." Not just needing all the socks and underwear to be lined up in a row in the dresser drawer, everything washed and ironed. "There was always sadness around her. But I wasn't going to ask. It was always, 'What are you talkin' about? I don't know what you're talkin' about.' My cousin, I do believe she committed suicide, but you couldn't get that outta them. They wouldn't say nothing."

Her mother lost her second-born baby, Michael, at six months, to pneumonia. Then Cully's father got tuberculosis and was confined to a sanitarium.

"They had those visits, you know? Connubial? That's how she got pregnant with me. So there was a big to-do about that! You know how nasty people can be. But, well, I'm just like my dad, so there was no more argument once I was born." Still, for some reason they moved to the Sarnia reserve, where Jenny was from.

Pierre: "I remember swimming in the crik down there, and there were frogs in there too." And watching television; black and white. "And you had to lean out the window to turn the antenna to get a channel from Detroit. I remember Mighty Mouse. I can still remember him flying up: 'Here I come to save the day!'"

One of Dudley's favourite TV characters was Dudley Do-Right, a lovable but not so bright RCMP officer who's always trying to save the woman he loves; that's where he got his nickname, Dudley.

But then the house burned down. Cully was fifteen, Pierre, twelve, and Dudley, eight.

Cully: "My whole house was gone, my identity! My mother used to have a trunk; I think it was from when she was in the army, and she kept things in there. She had this little red coat outfit, with a hat and everything. It was made out of red velveteen; I liked the way it felt. I remember I was wearing it once. It was my parents' anniversary and I was sittin' in the car pettin' it. It was my older sister Karen's (Jenny's first born), and her grandma had given it. Anyway, when the house burned down, it burned up that little coat and pants and everything that went with it."

The family was scattered for a while, staying in other family members' homes.

"I was always around my uncles and Grandpa ... They used a lot of Native stuff. It was just everyday life with them. You'd see them doing things like, even burning cedar on the stove. It *means* something if you burn cedar, or you burn sage or burn tobacco. Each of them have their own uses; the four medicines. You just watched and you learned. You just had to be around, and they'd be teaching you things. There was different other things that they showed me. Some of them are ceremonial, so I can't tell it here."

The family moved back to Kettle Point, which gave them a chance to go back to Stoney Point sometimes.

"It was our place again when we would go foraging – for morels and that. We couldn't do that in Kettle Point." But foraging was about all we could get away with. "If you wanted to make baskets, there was no land to get a tree from. Because the land was taken away from us."

Living what that meant – cut off from our land, our land overrun with young people learning how to be soldiers – was part of growing up for us; not just for Cully and Dudley but for Marcia and Glenn and the next generation too – Kevin, Marlin, and others.

Soon after Cully's family moved back to Kettle Point, their house there also caught fire. And Karen was killed in a car accident. Cully isn't sure which came first. By then, at sixteen, she had moved in with her boyfriend.

"I was just wantin' to get out of the house, because I felt I was more of a maid, to do all the work: the scrubbing, the laundry. The washing machine was down in the basement and you had to carry that load of laundry up the stairs and out to the yard.

"Mum was real bad after Karen died. Two kids, you know? Some people can't handle one. I don't think I could handle it, if my kids died ...

"She drank herself to death. The loss was too much."

Their father moved the family to Forest, with the high school close by and a place for Dudley to play hockey. But it wasn't easy juggling his schedule as a long-haul tanker truck driver. He took Pierre with him at least once.

Pierre: "We took one load [of diesel] up to Smooth Rock Falls [north of Timmins, north of Sudbury]. We had to drop off half the load someplace else and then we continued on north. There was nothing to look at; just evergreens way up north. That's not very interesting!"

Cully: "Dad had a hard time trying to keep all the kids together, behaving. Because he was a truck driver [and away overnight sometimes]. And, uh, me and Dudley – me, Pierre, and Dudley, we were the black sheep of the family."

Pierre: "We got a boot in the ass sometimes. But that's because we got caught doing something. Anything we shouldn't have been doing, we did it. Drinking beer, wine ... But that's the way it was for us. There was always booze. Always. Drinkin' ...

"I got four years of Grade 10. I got in trouble, eh? So I went to jail. But when I was there, I went to school. I got a diploma in commercial art." He still has some of his paintings.

Janet Cloud and her brother Maynard T. George grew up in a house moved from Stoney to Kettle Point too.

Janet: "They kept us secluded though, didn't want us to be involved with anybody around here. We couldn't go visit my next-door neighbour. If he [my dad] allowed us to go over there, it would only be for maybe ten minutes. And my mum couldn't talk to nobody. If anybody came to the house, she could only open the kitchen window so much and talk through there. I don't know if it was jealousy or if it was the move from Stoney Point. It could have been both."

But people came to them, and Janet listened in.

"I heard lots and lots of stories growing up. Not just by them but from other Stoney Point people. They were the real ones that were connected to the land because they were heirs of Waapagance. There was Auntie Liz and Johnny George. Sheldon Cloud, he was another one came to our house; different ones. And you'd hear the same stories. The same stories, and they'd laugh! When they talked in their own language, it was always laughter. Always enjoying their language. They never spoke to us in our language, but they'd talk to each other. And we picked it up anyway.

"My mother gave us all Native names. My brother Maynard, his Native name is Waapagance. Some people say it means mud and there is a mud crik that cuts through Stoney Point. But it means 'little piece of clay.' My name is Wakanse; that means 'wise.'"

After high school, Janet trained as a homemaker, to care for people, especially older people, in their homes. Maynard went to Sheridan College in Toronto to become a heavy-equipment operator, driving three hours each way every day to attend the classroom sessions. But then his car was struck by a fuel truck. He recovered the use of his legs, but not enough to carry on working.

Maynard: "I found the Lord and I was a lay preacher and then my mother wanted to go home so that's where my work here began – and I've been living it ever since." He started doing research on Stoney Point and our forced removal; he learned about the law and how to make depositions.

Bonnie grew up with her father Bruce saying, "C'mon, we're goin' to the bush today." He and Sheldon Cloud, "they were like brothers; they were very close." Sometimes they dug up saplings to sell to homeowners in the postwar suburbs going up around Sarnia. Bonnie's job was to tie a bit of old white cloth around a branch to mark which way was south. Often, as her father drove along scouting prospective buyers, he sent her to knock on the door and make the pitch. She was one of the first to attend high school, which was in Forest; though she had also been working since she was ten, walking cross-country to wash dishes at the Old Prices Ipperwash Hotel. One Saturday, in Sarnia, the man of the house asked Bonnie how much for the whole lot of trees. When Bonnie relayed the answer, he wanted to know how much all told if Bonnie's dad and his friend Sheldon would dig them all in as well. Okay, he said. They planted every one of the little trees they had in the back of the truck and got home early that day.

Every December, they slipped into our home reserve to cut Christmas trees plus cedar branches. Bonnie's mother Hilda and Sheldon's wife Jeannette worked these into wreaths on old coat hangers, the hooks making them easy to hang. On Saturdays, the women walked along the well-off streets of London, a bunch of plain wreaths on one arm, more expensive decorated ones on the other. Meanwhile, Sheldon and her father would have a burn barrel going in the market square, their trees arrayed beyond it.

Once, Bruce noticed a boy lingering among the trees and asked if he was looking to buy. "No, just lookin' to look," the boy replied. His family had never had a Christmas tree. So Bruce asked him how much money he had in his pocket. The boy fumbled around and came up with close to a dollar in change. His little brother found maybe a nickel in his pocket and added that.

"Well, I think we got some trees back here for a dollar. I'll show you where they're at," Bruce told the boy. Then, Bonnie recalls: "Sheldon, he talked real slowly. And he said, 'Eh Bruce, you keep this up, givin' everythin' away, I don't know if we're gonna make any money.' And those two kids are draggin' that tree down the street, goin' as fast as they could."

Mostly she remembers being with her father on their many excursions to Stoney Point. "He had an old black-assed pot. He wouldn't go into the bush without that pot. He always had tea and sugar too. Him and Sheldon would go back there and first thing they'd do, they'd go and get a few pieces of wood, make a tripod. Go and get fresh water out of the lake. Put it in there, boil it. Put tea bags in there. And those guys would sit there. They had those blocks of wood they used to sit on, and they'd sit on them, and I used to wonder, 'the hell do these old guys get from comin' back here?' And maybe every five minutes saying something. They'd be gawkin away, and they'd say, 'boy, I can hardly wait 'til we get back over here.'

"That was the issue with all these old people. They weren't asking for money. They were asking for their homeland back.

"I was just young when my dad, he would want me to go to meetings with him because I could write, and he would want notes. It was only when I was older that I realized what it was like, sitting on their land back in the bush. It's a feeling that don't come 'til you're older and you understand the meaning of the teachings about the land that was given to you ... and what the treaty meant: this is where we live, and we have laws. Our own judicial system here, that's my dream."

It was her father's dream to be buried at Stoney Point. "He used to joke about it: 'Well, Mum, if I go first, you remember, I go back to Stoney Point.' But he never – they didn't allow it." Still, Bonnie made sure he got a traditional send off, from his home at Kettle Point.

"His old friend Dunc came by, drunk as usual, and my uncle sent him away; told him to come back when he was sober. So I went out and asked, 'Did you come to visit Dad?'

"'Ya, that's what I was wantin' to do.' So I ushered him into the room where he was laid out, and I was listenin', and there was ole Dunc talkin' in there. Talkin' in the language and laughin'. I think I even heard Dad laugh, which was impossible. Dad was dead. And then Dunc come out, and he stopped in front of me. 'Thanks. I needed to talk with my friend before he leaves here.'

"They don't realize how strong our people are in the spirit world. And I know when I had my cancer, both times, it was my relations in the spirit world that got me through."

Bernard ("Slippery") George is from another branch of the George family and is also descended from one of Waapagance's sons. Most of the family lived in Kettle Point by then, but one of his grandmothers came from Stoney Point.

"It was always home to me." Growing up, he spent a lot of time at his grandparents' house. His mother had been in residential school and lost her language. "My grandfather spoke the language. He sang the language.

"You need the language to talk to the Creator." He learned a bit growing up, that's all. "It kinda fell asleep, but it's waking up now." He has sticky notes on all the different pieces of furniture in his home, each one with the Nishnaabemwin word for whatever the item is.

"When I went to school, I got punished because I didn't want to learn what they were trying to teach, by force: A, B, C, you know? One, two, three. They seemed to pick on me a lot. Why? Because I resisted? So it just led up to me not wanting to go to school. So the RCMP came and they dragged me out of the house and took me to school. It became a truancy thing in the courts. Because I didn't like the system. That system they had that was being forced upon me. And more and more anger came into me. I started hating on the system. And I wanted to fight with them because of what they were doing. I started damaging the school. And that put me in the training school system, and I was locked up in there. I seen a lot of bad things happen in there. I was slapped around in there and knocked around."

By sixteen, he had his first conviction: six months in jail for break and enter, with theft. Out on parole, he was convicted of common assault. Then he escaped custody and was charged for that. Next, it was for possession of stolen property. As the 1970s advanced, the charges and convictions continued: drunk driving, driving without a licence, failing to appear, robbery with violence, this one carrying a sentence of eighteen months.

Through all this, he could see the demonstrations happening outside the Ipperwash cadet training camp. Sometimes he took one of the leaflets being handed out.

"I knew it was our land. But I was still locked up inside. I was still into the drugs and alcohol.

"I had to get out of Kettle Point." He called his uncle Ted Bressette, who was a war vet. He told his uncle he wanted to take a tent and go hide out somewhere in the bush at the back of the army camp.

"He gave me a ride to Ipperwash Beach. We talked all the way down there. He told me, 'Don't be afraid. The military that's there, let them see you.' So I picked the highest sand dune, by the lake ..." And sure enough the military police showed up, "and they drove the jeep as high as they could, and they said they're gonna charge me with trespassing. So I told them, go get your commanding officer, and another jeep shows up. This guy had more stuff on his shirt. So I put my hands out. Go ahead, handcuff me. Throw me in jail. But I'm gonna keep comin' back.

"So, he says, 'How long do you intend to be here?' 'About a week ... just around here; maybe go down to the lake, catch a fish ...'

"They left me alone. But they watched me constantly. It was night and I could hear their radio goin'. I called to them: 'Come on up. I got an extra hot dog.' They moved away ..."

The days passed, and the nights he spent sitting in front of his fire. "I started thinking about my life: Am I goin' to keep doin' this? ... I felt really good. I was there with the spirits. I was talking to our grandfathers and our grandmothers ..."

By 1980, no further charges were laid against Bernard – until September 6, 1995.

Around the time that Bernard was camping out at Ipperwash, Ted Bressette's son, Tom, was serving in the US Army. Tom's great-great-grandfather was Oshawanoo, and his great-grandfather was Sam Bressette.[6] Sam was on the band council in 1927 when the chief and some others, including Sam, tried to stop our land being sold to a real estate developer. Tom's grandfather, also Tom, was chief for many years and helped organize the baseball team and a league with the other reserves. A lot of the young men in our families played on the Stoney Point team: Clifford George and his brother Ken, Daniel George, Reg, Abraham, Tom, and Bruce. They won lots of games. Tom's father, though, identified with being a soldier. "He raised me to be a soldier. He taught me what to do when you get up. How you do your work when you do it: you do it 'til it's done ... He raised me to be a get up and go-er."

Tom joined the army when he was seventeen and was sent to Fort Knox for training.

"They trained me to be an engineer when I went in there – the Army Corp[s] of Engineers. I learned how to build bridges, roads; how to lay mines and how to lift them."

He was sent to Vietnam when the war there was winding down and then to a base near Frankfurt in West Germany.

"I learned 'ein grosses Bier bitte.'

"I came back and things started to change! Uncle Sam had taught me." One of his first goals when he got elected chief of the band council was paving all the gravel roads on the reserve.

CHAPTER FOUR

Under Cover of Prayer Meetings

The people who were born on Stoney Point and many of us who are their children had been trying to get the government to return our land for years.

Rose: "The land was supposed to be returned. They emphasized that over and over again. It was just a temporary move in order to train their soldiers so they could go and win the war and come back and give us back our land."

A 1927 amendment to the Indian Act banned us from forming political organizations and even from hiring legal counsel.[1] Still, nothing prevented us from organizing a prayer meeting.

Marcia: "It was good cover." The church held a lot of power on the Kettle Point Reserve (and still does), but at least if you held a prayer meeting in your home, you were left alone. Someone would offer an opening prayer and then the people, sitting around in a circle, would start telling the old stories, sharing traditional knowledge, all in the language, our beloved Nishnaabemwin.

"They go hand in hand," the stories and the language they are rooted in, along with the feelings and the understanding that are woven into the stories and how words come together.

"My mother, she really took to the language." She had been cut off from it at residential school. "It was a way of trying, trying hard to say that this is a right ... It is indeed a beautiful rich language.

"And there were also efforts at teaching our Potawatomi heritage as well; they're all intertwined with our genealogies ... I started to get

51

my education with these old people. I really learned about what was important to me from these people."

Glenn: "They used to host meetings around the reserve, different houses. It was like a little social thing. They used to have coffee cakes and coffee and tea, that kind of stuff. And they used to always try and formulate some kind of plan on how they were going to get their land back through that system that's out there" in Ottawa. "They called themselves the Locatees."

The band office issued location tickets designating the particular part of the reserve land to which different families held use rights, though a lot of us Stoney Pointers had resisted this. As research for the Ipperwash Inquiry confirmed, location tickets were introduced by the government in the 1880s with the idea of introducing a more individualistic lifestyle around settled farming by subdividing the reserve. It was "quite an ambitious plan ... 'to civilize the Indians,' to get them to live in one place, become farmers, become Christians," according to some research Darlene Johnston did for the Ipperwash Inquiry. Joan Holmes added further insight from research she did: "People felt that they did not want their reserve subdivided, they wanted to maintain a kind of lifestyle and a land use and ownership system, which was more traditional to them, and in which individuals had ... a right to go around the reserve ... to use resources, to reside where they wanted to.

"So it becomes ... a bit of a struggle between maintaining a more traditional approach to land use and occupation or adopting the Indian Affairs regime of the subdivision of the reserve ... and the location system."[2]

That "bit of a struggle" got worse over the years as the government continued to impose more and more of their ideas on us, about who we should be and how we should live. Some people who got themselves elected to band council or got jobs in the band office were more willing to go along with the rules Indian Affairs set down. Others resisted, with some seeing this as assimilation – even colonization from the inside. It meant we weren't just divided and separated from so many of the things that made us Nishnaabeg. We were divided against each other. This threw a shadow over everything, especially as we organized among ourselves to get our homeland, Aazhoodena/ Stoney Point, back. But we kept at it.

Glenn: "All my brothers and my sister, they were part of those old locatee meetings where they used to talk about how these different

lands [including what became Ipperwash Park] were taken and why
... And I heard them talk about: 'maybe we got to serve them with an
eviction notice' ... And they wrote letters, you know, around the early
1970s, they wrote to all the politicians, whether they were at a provincial level, local level, or a federal level."

Bonnie's parents were part of these get-togethers, writing letters
and fundraising to hire a lawyer to go to Ottawa and fight for the return of our land.

Bonnie: "All the other kids could run around outside, but I had to
sit with my dad and take down notes. He'd tell me when to write. And
I seen them – all our people – all those years just get ripped off. Earning
money to pay a lawyer, and the lawyer would go to Ottawa and then
didn't get no place. Then we didn't have no lawyer. Then we'd find
another one, raise money again."

Rose: "They used to hold dances where my dad [Willington Elijah,
known as "Cob"], he used to call for those dances. And they would
charge so much per person to get in there. And they had box socials
and all different ways of making money, and of course going from
house to house and asking for donations of money to send somebody
to the government, to wherever they were – Ottawa."

In April 1972, Jean Chrétien, who was minister of Indian Affairs
back then, wrote a letter to his newly appointed counterpart in National Defence, Edgar Benson:

> The Indian people involved have a legitimate grievance. They did
> not agree to surrender the land in the first place, but it was appro-
> priated in the national interest prevailing in 1942. It is now 1972,
> and they have not got it back. Yet they desperately need it to improve
> the Band's social and economic position. In addition, there is their
> deeply rooted reverence for land and their tribal attachment to it.[3]

He acknowledged a stumbling block in all the unexploded munitions
said to litter the former reserve. At the time, the cost of cleanup was
estimated at between $18 and $30 million.

> They have waited patiently for action. There are signs, however, that
> they will soon run out of patience. There is bound to be adverse pub-
> licity about our seeming apathy and reluctance to make a just settle-
> ment. They may well resort to the same tactics as those employed by
> the St. Regis Indians at Loon and Stanley Islands in 1970 – to occupy

the lands they consider to be theirs. And as you know, Mr. George
Manuel, President of the National Indian Brotherhood, is interceding
on their behalf – he wrote to you on March 14 and sent me a copy.

Rose: "There was a lot of information that we received and always
a promise. But it was never carried through. They'd come by and say:
'Well, the government said this, the government said that, and, you
know, you have to wait a little longer.'

"But if one group quit, then there was another group that would
start right up; well, just on and off. They were always negotiating for
the return of Stoney Point."

But nothing changed. The government kept on denying us our right
– our collective treaty right – to live our lives on the land that has
always been the centre of our existence and where we were meant to
be. They didn't seem to understand how important this is to us – or
didn't care.

All around us, southwestern Ontario had changed – a lot. In 1942,
this area had been filled with family farms, largely self-sufficient like
we were at the time. And there were small towns with little craft-
scale dairies and cheese factories; furniture, farm implement, and
carriage making; seed mills and blacksmiths. We even had dealings
with some of them; the local ones. After the war, most of these little
operations disappeared. They were replaced by fewer and bigger ones.
A lot of these weren't locally owned anymore either. They were branch
plants of American multinational companies, and they were new industries too: chemicals and plastics and big factories making cars,
appliances, and farm machinery. There were still family farms around.
But there were more big commercial outfits, some specializing in crops
like corn, tomatoes, and tobacco. Even by 1961, 75 percent of Ontario's
population lived in cities, many living in postwar suburbs. Fewer than
10 percent lived on the land anymore, on farms.[4]

While all this change happened, we were still barred from deciding
for ourselves how to move forward. It was still against the law for us
to even go on our land.

Taking Things into Our Own Hands

Clifford George: "I was living in Sarnia when Maynard [T. George]
and his sister [Janet] started coming to see me about what are we

going to do to get the land back, because nobody was doing anything about it ... Maynard was very, very helpful at the start – the
start of the occupation. He helped us with a lot of archives work.
He went down there a week at a time to Ottawa to get some of the
archives."

Janet: "We weren't getting any answers, and the band council wasn't
helping us neither. And then we heard there was money for researching in the Ottawa archives. So we thought, well, let's go up there and
look for this archives thing. So away we went, two vanloads of us.
We didn't have no money. Everybody pulled their cash together, and
we went and did our *own* research.

"We couldn't believe it. Everything our parents had told us was in
there. Reel after reel. We couldn't get enough. We were lookin' and
reading. It was like a big light turned on. We stayed there three days,
and we would go to bed at three in the morning and get up at six and
go back again."

They didn't have enough support from the chief and the Kettle and
Stony Point band council to get an official band council resolution
that would give them access to the Red Series of documents. But the
head of the archives at the time gave access anyway.

"It was all about the military and how they got the people off their
property; all the things they did. We had people angry, crying. They
wanted to fight somebody. The heartache and the hardships they went
through in the move ... It was really hitting hard, hitting home what
they did to the people.

"But they put in there that the Indians are happy with the new
foundations when they moved to Kettle Point, and they didn't. They
[the houses that could be moved] were just set down there on boulders
and cinder blocks in the swamp! When my mum woke up in the morning and opened the door, salamanders went by."

The information they brought back from Ottawa got shared in strategy meetings and used in new pamphlets to be handed out at the next
protest. This was in the 1980s.

For Glenn, born in 1962, demonstrations were part of regular life
growing up. "It was always, 'Mum's going up there. You'd better get
out there and give her a hand.' 'Okay.'

"The military used to have this thing called LG Day [Lieutenant
Governor Day, when the lieutenant governor of the province came to
inspect the graduating cadets]. And they used to hand out information
to the public going by [parents of the cadets coming through the gate

onto the base]. A short little briefing about the history of the land, to raise awareness about the land being taken."

Marcia graduated from university (with a degree in administrative studies followed by a teaching diploma) and got a job as a teacher in London. She also got married and started a family of her own – all while she continued with the protests and searching out more information to support them.

"I have pictures of [Marlin and Kevin] holding placards when they were toddlers. And Mum made a big sign to put on Dad's hat. It said: '40-year loan is over.'"

One placard said: "WAR is over. We need our land" and another, simply "GIVE STONEY BACK." Some made reference to Tecumseh and Waapagance. Another one said: "We claim our land in the name of Jesus."

One time, we had a group called the Stoney Point Defence Committee, another time it was the Stoney Point Steering Committee, which later renamed itself the Stoney Point Community Association. The elders, though, always wanted to use the language; they called us simply *Aazhoodenaang Enjibaajig,* "the ones who come from Aazhoodena." Sometimes the chief and band council supported our efforts, depending on who was on council. A lot of the time, though, we were not sure we could trust them.

After Chrétien's failed attempts on our behalf, the National Indian Brotherhood stepped in and, together with the band office, started trying to negotiate something with DND. In 1980, they presented a proposal: a big government payout offer of over $2 million, supposedly as compensation for the government's use of our land and for our not being able to use it and live on it ourselves. Part of the money was to be distributed immediately and part put into a trust fund. But the money to be given out right away was to go to members of Kettle Point Reserve as well as us from Stoney Point. Why? Word got around that the two reserves might have been amalgamated at some point, which was news to us. The combined names started showing up on band office letterhead.

Janet: "All those years, they were just called Kettle Point, and all of a sudden when this money come in, that's when the letterhead changed."

We also worried that the government might treat this as a final settlement. One item in the proposal said that "When not required by Defence, parts or all of the Camp will be returned to us at no cost." And another clarified that the vote to accept the proposal was not a "surrender vote." Still, the phrase about the $2.49 million payout "representing additional compensation, interest and expenses" for our appropriated land had us worried. Might this be seen as something final? After the majority of the band members (Kettle Pointers as well as Stoney Pointers) voted in favour of accepting the offer, the defence committee organized a meeting at the baseball pitch, inviting government representatives to spell out what this vote accepting the payout meant. Someone thought we should make a tape recording of what was said, so we arranged that. This meant that when we asked for clarification, we got verbal assurances, on tape, that these moneys were only compensation for our being kept off our land since 1942, not compensation for the land itself; that is, not a sale.

Marcia: "They should have had an administration set up for Stoney Point to look after these things, but there wasn't one. We also did not like that the money was to go to the people of Kettle Point as well as the ones originally from Stoney Point. We staged a protest outside the gates of our homeland to make this public."

That is about when the Stoney Point Steering Committee got started. One of its objectives was to lobby Indian Affairs and other government departments to ensure that we Stoney Pointers were "recognized as the legal heirs and negotiating body in any return of Camp Ipperwash."

We also drafted a petition to formally separate ourselves from Kettle Point, and a lot of our people signed it.

The demonstrations outside the army gates continued, with Melva and Daniel George still in the forefront, helping to keep it all going. But Daniel's emphysema was getting worse. So he brought a lawn chair and sat on it holding his sign. Melva started bringing a chair too and sat beside him with her sign.

In the late 1980s, some elders approached Bonnie to run as band council chief. She had dropped out of high school to help her parents financially, working as a short-order cook in a restaurant, then in the Forest Basket factory, which supplied wicker baskets to the big food-processing plants operating in the area, like Del Monte and Campbell's. She worked on some of the farms, too, topping turnips and pulling carrots for so much a bushel. And she had taken a business administration correspondence course, borrowing a typewriter so she could type up her work while keeping an eye on her four children. When she was first elected as a band councillor, in 1969, she'd also taken on the newly created position of economic development officer as well as welfare administrator.

"We were so tired of being on our knees all the time with Indian Affairs, begging for the right to deliver services in our community. 'Give us the money; we can do it better than you can.' This one guy, he used to almost boast, 'Hell, I make enough off my travel allowance to live on ...'

"We just decided, we're not gonna put up with this shit anymore. You had to put up with it [before] because they'd call in the Mounties if you bothered the Indian agent."

She started applying for federal and even provincial grants, first to build a daycare at Kettle Point so the women could get the schooling they needed to get a decent job, then to start a small-business training program for community members, then to build a fire hall, a new band office, plus a plaza with a supermarket and restaurant on the reserve. She went to Ottawa with a delegation of regional and local chiefs when the federal government came out with its "Canada Jobs Strategy" in the early 1980s. "It included training, helping people get into self-employment ... They set aside 7 percent of their budget for minorities, Aboriginals – no, we were 'Indians' at the time – plus women and disabled."

They sat outside the minister's office for four days because the minister of Employment and Immigration was too busy to meet with them. Eventually, the minister, Lloyd Axworthy, ushered them in and listened to their proposed changes. "And he said, 'I totally agree with you; we will make those changes.'"

"When I was chief, I only went to two meetings in Ottawa for the return of the land, and every time I went there I could not get to see anyone. I just got to see the inside bureaucrats; I didn't get to see anybody that could give me a yes or no answer."

She decided to try another approach. She contacted the CBC's *Fifth Estate,* a popular news-documentary television program.

"I made a couple of calls. I was always one that was never afraid to try anything once. I can't even remember the people I talked to. I told them, 'You know, them people are still down there, and they're robbin' our jobs.' It was after I'd bid on so many contracts. You couldn't even get a friggin' cleaning contract in there. They only took on token Indians in the summer. And I told them, 'they've got this Marriage Patch [a mini campground next to Ipperwash Provincial Park on a bit of the army camp that gave onto a nice stretch of beach]. And this old retired colonel come down, brought the wife down, got the kids down, and they worked in the kitchen. And the colonel and his wife had these big swanky trailers. And here, the Marriage Patch was all serviced with hydro, water, the whole bit [from the provincial park] – for a dollar a day!

"Everybody's vacationing free on my family – and my family is everybody at Kettle and Stoney Point whether they look at it that way."

In the summer of 1989, a film crew from *The Fifth Estate* drove to Ipperwash to check out the tenting and trailer park tucked away at the back. They called it a "military Club Med."

Host Bob McKeown interviewed one of its happy campers, an air cadet officer with his bare belly red from the sun, who told McKeown: "It's a home away from home on weekends, relaxation and such. We're not goin' to give it back to anybody really." The documentary ends with Bonnie likening what happened in 1942 to people being evacuated in an emergency. "We were evacuated for military purposes, but some day we're going to go home."

Within months of "A Hell of a Deal" being aired, the Marriage Patch was shut down. But that's all. Roofers were seen putting fresh shingles on some of the barracks. The protests continued.

Rose: "Our older people wanted to go home, and this is why we were demonstrating and doing everything we could. There was nothing else to do.

"We'd tried everything. We tried letter writing, talking to government officials; we tried everything to get our land back. Everything that we could possibly try, we tried it, and they just turned a deaf ear.

"They had their own agenda, and our agenda was always to go back to our home. Because it was our land. It was our home. It was everything to us. It wasn't just a piece of property out in nowhere. It was where we were happy. And this is why we were doing what we were doing. And it was for everyone, because our older people couldn't do anything anymore, but they wanted to return to their homeland. They wanted to enjoy their last few years in their homeland and also to look after the burial grounds. And when my dad was passing away, I promised him that I would continue to fight to get back our homelands."

In the summer of 1990, some of our younger Nishnaabe travelled to Kanesatake in solidarity with the Mohawks in their seventy-eight-day standoff with the Quebec Provincial Police and the Canadian army over Indigenous burial grounds that the town of Oka wanted to turn into a golf course. Some time that year, too, Parliament's Standing Committee on Aboriginal Affairs issued a statement that "the government [must] rectify a serious injustice done to the Stoney Point First Nation ... by returning the land at Stoney Point to its original inhabitants and their descendants from whom the land was seized."[5] It had no effect.

That fall, Daniel George, who was Melva's husband, Marcia and Glenn's father, and Kevin and Marlin Simon's grandfather, passed away.

The family made a plea to be allowed to bury Daniel at Stoney Point, with Graham, the oldest, meeting directly with senior officials at the army base. When permission was granted, Glenn arranged for his father's and mother's nephews to act as pallbearers, including Reginald's son Dudley. Marcia thought the media should know and asked her cousin Maynard T. George to help.

Marcia: "I had this great big administrative studies book and it had some information about doing up a press release. It had a neat format that was easy for someone to follow. It was really helpful that way."

It was the first burial on the reserve since 1942. And many people came, following Daniel George's coffin as he took a last ride around Stoney Point to the place where his and most of the rest of our ancestors were buried. Renewing the connection.

Janet: "It was a real surprise to me that they were taking him home to Stoney Point to be buried; that never ever happened before. I thought that was really something; it was like a beginning."

There were so many people who came, the funeral procession filled the road that went around the reserve. Cars were still coming in the gate when the first ones started parking at the base of the burial grounds.

Kevin: "It was the first time for many people, getting to ride around the reserve. It gave them a taste for coming home."

Marcia: "When they saw Dad going home, they wanted it too. People would come up to me and say: 'maybe we can live in our homeland again.'"

A few people noticed the eagle in the sky. It seemed to hover over the procession all the way to the burial grounds. Kevin had dreamed of an eagle shortly before his grandfather died.

CHAPTER FIVE

Burying the Hatchet
under a Peace Tree

May 6, 1993

D aniel George's burial deepened the other elders' longing to move back home and our determination to get them there. The day it finally happened, getting into the Ipperwash army base was easy. The elders – most of them well into their seventies – would go for a picnic.

Janet: "We had a little meeting. The elders said, 'tomorrow,' so Maynard worked all night doing up a press release. We were to go and fax it off to the various places – the DND, the local MPP, the police; every person Maynard could think of. It was from people's telephones that we faxed it out" as soon as the elders went in.

Rose: "We went through the front gate. We had a little carload ... with Clifford driving and I asked them if we could go in; we were going to camp for the day. They said, 'Sure, go ahead; there's no problem. Just go and have a picnic and stay for the day ... Go under the trees over there in that little orchard.'

"But I felt that was too close to the army camp, so I said: 'Let's go on the range.'" In other words, the rifle ranges. They were a ways away from the built-up part of the army camp and also close to where many of our homesteads used to be. "And so we went right in there, and it's where our first camp was.

"But on the outside, there was Maynard T. George and Carl George, and they were photocopying papers; eviction papers for the military.

They'd told us, just go on in and park somewhere and we'll come along later and give those papers to the right people."

Janet: "Dolleen [Rose's daughter] and I were handing out papers. We faxed them to all the important people, the higher ups."

This was our plan: to repossess our homeland; to serve the army people with an eviction notice so we could live here, in our own way, again.

Clifford: "We'd discussed what's the best way to do this, because it had been dormant and nobody was doing anything ... and we were getting sick and tired of nothing happening."

The most recent setback had been in 1992. In March, the Standing Committee on Aboriginal Affairs tabled a report recommending that the Camp Ipperwash lands be returned. In August, DND responded saying they needed to continue to retain the lands, but they agreed to consult with the First Nations people.[1] So, nothing but more talk.

The notice we sent to the OPP and the local Member of Provincial Parliament (MPP), Marcel Beaubien, was signed by Carl O. George as acting chief and Maynard T. George as acting councillor.[2] It began: "We have come here in the name of our people, tradition and custom ... We are not claiming Stoney Point Reserve (#43) in the name of only those uprooted but also in right of the first, second and third generations of children whose parents and grandparents have been victimized by the taking of their land (farms) in 1942."

It was still early in the morning and Rose at least had not even had breakfast yet. But in their first action as their own self-governing Stoney Point community, they issued a first statement. "Be it known thereafter that we are repossessing our homelands called Aazhoodena and the territory of our people." Some people went around posting little notices about this on fence posts, too, announcing that the elders have reclaimed Stoney Point as our homeland.

Rose: "I think Maynard was the one that was the brains behind all that. He had been visiting local archives as well as the one in Ottawa. He said he had done all this research and he finally found the loophole to get in there, so no one would bother us; no one could kick us out."

It's called "colour of right," he said. It means that if we honestly feel we have a right to be here, we are not committing a crime like trespassing.

Rose: "And it was all to be done in a peaceful manner, and we wouldn't be using any guns or any form of harassment."

Clifford: "The purpose was to occupy our lands peacefully, eventually to see if we can get it legally back into our own hands as Stoney Pointers."

Marcia: "We hoped to start – jump start some sort of negotiations where we would officially have our land returned and recognized as ours."

Meanwhile, we intended to live in our homeland again, which is what our elders wanted.

Janet: "We were just innocent people. We didn't know all the legalities. We didn't know nothing. All we knew is that 'we're takin' them home.' That was my vision: it was to see my mum go back home.

"Oh my mum! She's sitting in the middle of the field there. She had some material and she's sewing away; fixing something. And she was so happy! And Cliff, you could see the twinkle in his eye. 'We're home; we're home. I never thought I'd see this day – to come home.' That's all that mattered to them.

"They were so happy. You could see it. It's in their eyes. It's in their walk. It's in their lookin' around. It's in their actions. All of a sudden they took command. Cliff took command. My mum took command. This is their home. This is their land. 'I'm here; nobody's movin' me.'

"The military tried to serve us same as we did with them, with an eviction notice. They came and served our babies, and Mum said: 'we ain't movin nowhere,' and she never did."

Marcia: "I was there to stay. Not necessarily on the spot where we were at [that day]; later on that summer we moved to my great-grandfather's estate. But still, I felt the whole property was mine, or shared amongst our Nation."

People explored around, finding blooming hyacinths where different families' homesteads had been. One of the elders spotted a broken line of fading daffodils – it signalled where our old schoolhouse once stood.

Someone rigged up a tripod for cooking where the Elijah homestead had been. Abe, the only one of the group that had been old enough to have his own place and location ticket in 1942, had an old tarp he and some others used when they went hunting. He rigged this up as cover. Soon we had a fire going.

Janet: "I remember Marlene [Cloud] making fry bread on top of the fire. She was making bannock, that very first day that we moved in. Maynard said: 'Start cooking. Fry up some onions. Make it smell like home, like we're having our supper.' We were doing all the things we had to do to get established right there. We're home now is what we said. Just start being at home."

Glenn got back to his mother Melva's place (at Kettle Point) after a day installing fire hydrants around the Kettle Point Reserve, "and my mother had all these sandwiches and cakes, and these coffee thermoses; and she had tea and coffee, she had water, and she had all this stuff all packaged up. And she told me: 'Marlin and Kevin are in there. You better go look after them.'

"So I went down there, and when I got there it was, there was a lot of people that, you know, were kind of viewing how they were going to spend the night. And they had this, this look about them: 'You're not going to leave, are you?' They're hinting around that ... So I stayed with them."

Marlin: "My brother was going to school in London and I was at his place ... and we seen it on the news, so right after we got done eating, we jumped in his truck and went down there to go see what was going on, and then I ended up staying there ever since ... I wasn't really doing anything at the time. I think I dropped out [of school]; Grade 11, I think."

Kevin: "The [elders] called it their homecoming, because they knew they're at the end of their life and all their life they were told if they were to try to come in there and try to do this thing before, basically they could have been shot dead. End of their lives? They didn't care. They were goin' home. And since that was my grandma there, one of those [elders], we wasn't goin' to let that happen. So we followed them in ... back to their homesteads."

Some had little pup tents. Some slept that first night in cars or the back of their pickup trucks.

Rose: "It was nice when we arrived but it come up a north wind, and we were pretty cold, and they had the younger people making a fire for us. But even though we sat around with blankets over us, I was still cold. I had to crawl back into my car, and I started the car every little while."

Janet: "Then people started bringing in trailers because we had to get out of the elements, when it rained or whatever. We had to have shelter for our elders. Each one began to have trailers."

One of the things Maynard had included in the notices we sent out was that: "We are not hindering the elected Kettle Point Council or people from joining us, but *they do not represent us* in any way, shape or form."

Clifford: "We didn't trust them all that much because – for several reasons. He [band council chief Tom Bressette] wasn't doing nothing about it [helping us reclaim the Stoney Point Reserve]."

Marcia: "He used to run us down in the media, what we were doing."

The next day, Tom Bressette and the band council met, passed a resolution, and issued their own press release, saying: "we do not sanction the occupation ... [we] are satisfied that our discussions with the federal government are progressing." The release went on to list several points, including: "Claims of malicious treatment towards the people from Stoney Point who were moved to Kettle Point in 1942 are unjustified."

Meanwhile, we were starting to settle in and make ourselves at home beyond the barracks and built-up area of the army camp, getting on with what we considered important. This included deciding how we were going to govern and police ourselves.

Clifford: "One thing we made plain when we decided to walk in there was no weapons, because most of these people, they still hunt for a living. So their weapons were left at the reserve [Kettle Point]."

Marcia: "We were very adamant that we would be nonviolent."

Kevin: "We had a tree-planting ceremony. We call it the Peace Tree.[3] It's a pine tree. Underneath that tree, we buried the hatchet, and it was symbolic of how we were going to live out our occupation of these lands; that we weren't there to be troublemakers ... We were there just to, to raise awareness of what was happening – to jump start some sort of negotiations where we could officially have our land returned and recognized as ours ... And through that ceremony, we were able to show our intent – to each other and to outsiders, that we didn't mean nobody harm."

Everybody took a turn digging the hole in which to bury the hatchet, Dudley included.

Clifford: "There was several make-believe [plastic] hatchets there, that everybody had a chance to throw in, in this deep hole that we dug, to throw in the hatchet, and we buried it."

Pierre: "I made some hatchets too. Went in the bush, cut some sticks ..."

Kevin: "And my Auntie Cheryl, she married Darryl Stonefish – he's from Moraviantown, down by the Thames; they brought a black stone pipe. It was one of those hatchet-pipe combinations. It was the real deal. So part of the ceremony to bury that was to make it known to everybody that we were doing what we were doing in a peaceful manner. We were burying that black pipe; the war pipe was what that was. You have your red peace pipe with the good red road and peaceful living, and the other's not so much."

Marlin: "At first we were just sittin' around waiting for something to do. And Uncle Abe, he showed me where the well was. And we were playing around with those old divining rods. We used a forked stick the first one, and there's another where you bend two pieces of wire. We ended up finding where the spring was. So we put a flagpole up, on that spot ... After that, he said we needed a cookhouse. My uncle Glenn had given us a bunch of tarps, old military tarps. And then we made like an A-frame structure, and we used those tarps; fastened on at the end. And we went and gathered up a bunch of their wooden platforms that they used for serving the cadets [outside]. So we gathered up a bunch of those and made a floor for our little cook shack."

Marcia: "They scrambled around to get things. My youngest, Kevin, had a red Nissan truck. And I remember running around trying to find a topper for it so at least he could sleep in the back of the truck ... There was still frost on the ground, and I had concerns. I didn't want them getting sick.

"And I knew the importance of having better facilities [than tents]. So I shopped around for some old used camper trailers, and [using her lump-sum summer teacher's pay] I purchased two of those and that one week we moved them onto our grandparents' estate."

Glenn: "[I'd had] about all that I could handle because the council [at Kettle Point] was kind of giving me the runaround because I was working on the reserve and I was living on the camp, and then, I don't know, I guess my priority was more to helping those people at the camp than it was running a construction crew.

"I remember at the time I went in, I seen my uncle Abe and I asked him, I want you to show me exactly where this homestead was, because I didn't want to get into that part of bickering about who lived where and stuff like that ... And people needed that too, you know, people that had this knowledge right then and there, to have that witness I guess ... That's when my uncle Abe came with me. He showed me where the house was, where the barn was, where the shed was, where the well was. And he said, right then and there he says: 'You've got to dig that well out.' Like, the army filled in our whole homestead well ... And I feel kind of like a hypocrite; I was told to do something and it, it hasn't been done yet."

Marlin: "Uncle Abe ... It was like he was in heaven. He would go and cut wood for the cook fire. He ended up getting a sacred fire going there after a while, too."

Marcia: "And he would sit there and look after it if there was nobody else around to do it."

Kevin: "Usually a sacred fire is just a few days. But that one we kept going [for nine months] because I guess we all knew that what we were doing was special. What's happening here is happening all across Turtle Island – actually all around the world. Colonials went everywhere, took land, lied, cheated, stole."

Marlin: "It was a place where people offered their prayers and tobacco and whatever; their offerings. And my role in it was fire keeper: go out and cut wood, keep the fire going, and just look after the grounds where the fire is. [Others] would be my brother Kevin, Dudley, Pierre, Warren, Glenn. There were others [from other reserves]. If they couldn't be there during the week then they'd come along on the weekend and help out."

Cully: "We had the [sacred] fire. Everybody sat around it. You could put your tobacco down and nobody was gonna look at you funny. You felt more normal here.

"Uncle Abe was there; he was just like my father. He told us about the time he got pneumonia, and they had to walk to Thedford to get the doctor, and the doctor came in a sleigh drawn by horses. And he told about the surgery.[4] They done the surgery right on the table; he was having trouble breathing. He almost died, but he got saved ... And he told about going in the bush to get logs. He come back and he thought the water [through the swamp] was ice and then the horse broke through, and he had to do his darndest to get that horse out of there. He said, 'I had to lift him by his head to pull him up.'"

Abe sat by the fire a lot too because of his emphysema. Plus, he had only one lung, ever since he had pneumonia. But he knew the bush at Stoney from all the woodcutting and trapping for furs he'd done when he was young. So he could tell everyone where to find a stand of ash that you could burn in the fire green. His daughter Joy Lewis visited him when she could, but only over the fence.

Joy: "I wasn't allowed in there because I was working for the army at the time. Me and my brother Rod[erick], 'Judas.' ... It would be conflict of interest sort of. So I'd visit him over the fence, and he'd tell me what he'd done during the day. And they had a place for him to sleep. They kept him fed. He was always talkin' about homemade bread and soup. He made a lot of friends from other reserves too."

Bernard George, now a band councillor, brought a tent and his family and camped out some weekends that summer. Bonnie Bressette, still on band council herself, brought her grandchildren.

"And I remember Uncle Abe telling me, 'You don't know what it feels like to be back on your own land – after all those years of sneaking around.'

"And [since then], I can go down to my Mum and dad's homeland [down near the park], and there isn't a place I feel safer ... I have a strong belief in the spirit of my mother and my dad and my aunts and my uncles [being there]."

Glenn: "We had a cook shack, eh? It had a tarp and we had a tripod for cooking over an open fire, and we had propane cookers, like out of a trailer."

Marcia: "It was like having a propane range in your house, and we had these outside there. It was really nice."

Glenn: "And we had a [school] bus given to us by my brother [Warren] and he was going to use it for storing, and I remember my nephew [Harley] was going to use that for his living quarters, and there was tents. It was like tent city. There was lots of tents, and I think ... the bailiff had a couple of trailers. I don't know if he was repossessing them or if they would just give them to him. But I helped dismantle them and get them roadworthy to drag them down the road."

The bailiff was Scott Ewart. He lived up the road near Grand Bend; his wife had written letters in support of us over the years. At one of the meetings of our Stoney Point council, we appointed Mr. Ewart to act on our behalf. He helped us with the kind of legal language he used in his work as a bailiff, and we used this in different documents. The first of these, which was delivered by hand to the base commander, served notice to them "to not resist or willingly obstruct the legal seizure and repossession of the lands herein named." The second, addressed to the Department of National Defence and delivered on June 9, 1993, went further. It served notice under the Trespass to Property Act that the Canadian army was trespassing on First Nations territory.

Clifford: "And that was delivered to the camp commander. He came out to the gate. We had several people there. And we asked him to come out to our meeting, and he did, and he accepted."

More and more media came. Items appeared on local radio and TV news, and articles appeared in the Sarnia paper and the *London Free Press.*

The Hunter brothers, local hockey players, donated a trailer. Hydro workers in Sarnia donated two.

Clifford: "One was a really nice trailer and we [the council, by now elected] decided to give it to Dudley [because he was always there]. It was the first home he ever owned, and he was very proud of it."

Dudley found a board, painted it, and turned it into a sign for the trailer: "Dudley's Place," he called it.

Janet: "So many unions helped us out – United Steelworkers, CAW [Canadian Auto Workers]. Buzz Hargrove [union president at the time] came to see us – in the middle of the field! And we had the president of the Japanese Canadian Association, and he had people demonstrating with us because they had the War Measures Act too; it was imposed upon their people. We did talks too."

One was to the Friends of the Aboriginals in Stratford. "They were businessmen from Stratford, and there was teachers in amongst them, and a psychiatrist. They wanted to support us, so they donated. And there was a producer with the singer Loreena McKennitt. Loreena McKennitt sent us a thousand dollars."

Clifford: "Different organizations, Christian organizations, some of them raised money through bingos and this and that to help us out on the reserve because we could not draw no compensation, no nothing nowhere.

"Even a food bank refused us – some of our people – food. And I come to them, to Forest, and I exposed to them that they have no business denying anyone. I don't care who it is; that's what the food bank is for, and they got very flustered."

Rose: "There was supporters from different reserves, and they would visit different ones of their relatives or they would bring in food ... My boys had to continue to work and so they supported us through bringing food in. And the people that came to visit, they brought in food, and blankets, and different things. Because we were living there with nothing except for the donations that came in."

Tom Bressette: "There were, I guess, some accusations going on. He [David Henry, welfare administrator for the Kettle and Stony Point band office, at Kettle Point] was withholding assistance or whatever. And he has the regulations that state where people have to be, and our jurisdiction at that time was clearly outlined as the First Nation land boundaries. And if people were living [off the reserve land itself] he would deny them."[5]

Kevin was out of work for a time: "I had no income whatsoever. So I went and asked for welfare, but I was told that Chief Tom Bressette had gone and said: 'We look after our own.' So if I wanted welfare, I had to go back to Kettle Point; Kettle Point won't give welfare unless you're living on the reserve, which we were not. So, no welfare for me! So I fished in the lake out here; set nets. Different people would help. It's how I was raised – [work] bees. My grandfather and Uncle Abe, they would hunt together, and share."

By then, he was sleeping in a shed by the road leading to the rifle ranges. "It was just a small shed; nothing really fancy about it. It was green, maybe twelve feet by sixteen. And there was a bench around the wall inside and a small oil furnace in the middle. It had a sign on the door as you went in. It said 'Shelter.' So, I needed some shelter.

"I had a table and chairs and a couple of couches I used for a bed. Clothes, alarm clock, and stuff."

The Auto Workers donated lumber and plywood. Some used it to build sixteen-by-sixteen-foot shacks or front-ends onto their trailers. Clifford rigged up a wood stove in the fancy little one he built on his family's former homestead. He made a sign for it too. He called it: "Uncle Cliff's Cabin."

STONEY POINT REVIVED

A lot of the donated wood went into building our first gathering place as a community. It was just a small building made of two-by-fours, plywood, and particle board. But it was raised up by all of us sharing the work in a building bee.

Kevin: "It was great. It was going to be our band office ... Everyone kind of pitched in with what they had. Glenn brought some windows and framing his father had set aside for building a garage some day ... Everybody did what they could. Everybody was happy. We were proud of what we were accomplishing."

Clifford: "One of the boys [Victor George] was a carpenter, and he put a steeple on that building, and it was all across Canada because

I heard from BC, 'Did you really do that? Your first building was a church?'"

Marcia: "That was so upsetting; that it got all across Canada that that's what it was called. The people were not consulted about the media doing that."

It was not long before the steeple was gone.

Kevin: "It got torn off."

Janet: "It was built for a church, and they knocked our steeple down."

Kevin: "Eventually, they started calling it the Argument Hall, because you couldn't have a meeting without people getting angry. There were ones, I think they were coming from a band office state of mind, where they're trying to secure the funding, like the grass-cutting contract [with the DND, held by the Kettle Point band office]. There's always other people's agenda. We'd try to have a meeting on how we were going to move forward in dealing with DND in a peaceful manner, and it always seemed that we could never get to that. Somebody would show up, and they would have an issue and that would be the end ... My mum [Marcia], she offered to be – what did she call it? Elections officer. She was in charge of tellin' people to shut it when they wanted to raise a ruckus: 'That person shouldn't vote' or whatever ... Everybody was going back over their family trees. I think it was twenty-two families that were originally removed in 1942. And we kind of decided that those should be the ones that make up the community – not the ones that had lived someplace else and had a woodcutting lot."

Cully's name was on the list: "Someone come and said, we need you, and I thought, what better chance to go? I'd just broke up with my husband. I think he thought I was his meal ticket. But I just got hit too many times, and I finally got tired of it. And I didn't think it was right for the kids to put up with that."

When she arrived, the first thing she did was flop down on the ground and make a snow angel in the grass. "I'm home; I'm home," she called out loud. "This is where I was supposed to grow up."

Cully: "This is where I can be who I want to be. Like, I had come home. It took me a long time to get here, and, 'Dad, you didn't make it, but I know you're watchin' us and you're glad we're here.' Because all of them had pretty much given up because they couldn't get nowhere to get the land back. They had no place to live in, no place of their own. A lot didn't want to live in Kettle Point. And a lot were enfranchised."

She headed to the cooking area. "We had a gas stove hooked up, and an ice box; a great big one, a fisherman's one. And we'd get water to do dishes ... And I was doing a lot of the cooking. You get up in the morning, go over, and you start cooking, and the people would gather ... and have coffee ... I was more into making sure there was food and the place was cleaned up and not into so much of how the place was run.

"I'd worked down there at the [Ipperwash] camp [as a teenager, like Marcia and Rose's daughters: in the kitchens and dining halls that had names like the Savoy, the Ritz, the Trocadero]. And they would get mad, 'Oh, you can't go there. You can't walk there.' I thought, 'This is my land!' I couldn't say that to the MPs [military police] when the army was here."

Marcia: "They went out hunting this one night, I'm not sure where, and they came home empty-handed, and I had to go to work the next day [teaching school in London]. On my way home, this nice little black car ahead of me ran over a deer. He was really shaken; he'd almost lost control of his car and everything, and the old deer is lying there. So I asked him if he wanted it ... So we loaded it on the trunk of my car and tied it down with bungie cords and took it to our campsite. And when we turned in there, you could hear Cully laughing. How silly that could be: I went to work and brought home a deer and our hunters came home empty-handed."

Marlin: "I chopped it up, hung it up overnight ... and we got it all cleaned up, all the bad meat cut away. Braised it all up into little stewy bits and handed it out ... Everybody had a little bit ... It was pretty neat. I was kind of used to living outside ... Setting up camps and stuff like that was normal ... It made you happy; like, my grandfather [Daniel George] had always talked about Stoney Point."

Cully: "There were more women here, too. So it was more fun. We'd be bad! We'd take off and have a few beers. Then we'd go down to the lake and throw water on us, 'Yeah, we just went swimming.'

"And since Dudley was there at Stoney Point when they asked me, 'Do you want to come and check it out?' I figured it would be okay ... Dudley had stayed at my place different times and I was close to him ... We were the black sheep of the family. Just because we were smoking grass and drinkin'. I guess all of them did drink. But it was the grass they didn't like.

"He was very close to my kids [including Glen Bressette, known as J.R.], almost like a father figure. I was the only parent there, and I was the one who had to lay down the law and stuff, and if they were upset, they would go to him. They would talk to Dudley and Dudley would help smooth it out ... Dudley was a person who could always make you feel good ... He would make you laugh ... And he was always willing to help out. I mean, not willing, but he would."

J.R.: "He was fun to hang out with. He'd come down and watch *The Simpsons* with us. He loved Bart Simpson. He loved that show. And he loved movies with Indians in them." His two favourites were *Dances with Wolves* and *Little Big Man* with Chief Dan George.

Marlin: "Dudley and I, we hung out together. Just a bunch of young guys ... Got on each other's nerves, bust each other's balls, I guess. Ended up having to babysit the guy when he'd get too drunk. We'd always be laughing at him, teasing him – 'tipsy' – when he'd get too drunk, he couldn't stand up.

"He was just a small guy. Comical. He was a fun guy to be around ... I remember, they were always telling the army to leave, or get lost, or take a hike, or whatever ... Dudley would be ridiculing the [military] police ... in different kind of ways. Maybe shooting a finger or whatever."

It was kind of funny too, considering that Dudley got his nickname off that old TV cartoon character Dudley Do-Right, an RCMP cop.

Marcia: "He was the heart of our community, that crazy ole Dudley. He was almost like a clown. He would tell jokes that were old and stale, and he'd laugh hardest himself ... Dudley's trailer became a focal point. They got a woodstove set up in there and a long table. Big pots of soup with dumplings would be taken in there for the guys. People who'd come to find out about Stoney Point, that's where they'd come as well. And our other cousin, Warren, he'd stay there too. [Dudley was] not a leader. He was just silly ... Everybody loved him ... He was right there in support of everything. And if ever they would do a ceremony, he was very respectful of those things, and he was right there to take part in them as well."

Gina Johnson, like Kevin, was only sixteen at the time, "and my brother Bernard [George] said, 'let's do it.' I'd always known I was a part of Stoney Point [and a descendant of Waapagance, the Ojibway chief who represented Aazhoodena when the Huron Tract Treaty was negotiated], and there was this crazy pride in knowing that you're from here. At the time, I didn't drink. I didn't do drugs. I was sober for many years. I would come down here quite often, playing cards in people's trailers at night, helping with cooking during the day, and going to the meeting hall. I was there at every meeting that I could get to – at the old Argument Hall.

"We all ate together. We all cooked together. We came together as a community, and we were united. We were all fighting for the same thing: just to get our land back ... It was, okay, we'll listen to this person, and pass the feather around, and everyone would have a say in what's going on. And it was also practical stuff, like Elwood's out of wood; we'll have a work bee ... That's when the occupation was still civil, when it was still just saying 'We're not goin' anywhere.'"

We stayed in the area east and north of the barracks and built-up area. It was near the bush but also right next to the rifle ranges. The ranges were still being used on a regular basis, though at least they used that little red flag to warn us. The MP came by on their regular patrols, twice in the day, and twice at night too. And the teaching officers still took cadets on runs and marches past where we were camped and living.

Marcia: "We would see the military jogging down the road singing those sounds, and armed. People were terrified of that because they didn't know what they were planning to do ... And there were times when the grenades would be going off ... blasting so loud! I just felt that they were really hurting the earth with those things. Poor old earth."

Sometimes they yelled things at us, like "Wahoos!" and "Pay your taxes!" And sometimes we yelled things at them, like "Get off our land!"

Marlin: "Most of the time, it was just kind of taunting each other. Kind of like neighbours bickering at each other all the time."

Cully: "There was some guys there drinking, and one guy, it was Stewart [George] I think, he threw a beer bottle at the patrol going by [in an open jeep], and he hit the back tire. And the MP got all excited and he says, 'you were trying to hit me,' and I just went over there and told him: 'If he was trying to hit you, he would have hit you. He's got a good aim.'"

One night toward dawn, Kevin's dog started to growl.

Kevin: "So I had a look, and it was the army coming ... They had those big army trucks with the canvas back on them and a couple of more the range patrol type trucks. And they come up there with no lights on. As soon as they seen me, noticed I was awake, they turned on their lights, and they backed up to the side of the shed where I had the fridges and stoves ... The spot where I was working at the time, in London, was a three-storey walk-up. They were basically throwing out all the appliances in there, and I tried a few of them out, and they still worked. I figured, why not? I brought them down, maybe half a dozen fridges, half a dozen stoves. I had them piled up around outside ... to give them to people. We were getting generators brought in, and I figured sooner or later people will be able to use them as we made ... permanent homes.

"Guys jumped out of that big truck and started loading up those fridges and stoves, and other people, whatever vehicle they came out of, they basically just came in a line at me at the door. I asked what was going on. And they said they were here to clean out their building. I told them my view on the building. I considered it mine, seeing as it was on my land.

"They said they didn't have no question about whose land it was, but they knew it was their building. So I basically told them to take their building; get it off our land. They said they couldn't do that, and they physically pushed their way in ... I was outnumbered, and they were a lot bigger than me."

They took everything away, including his clothes and alarm clock. He never saw any of it again. When he got home from work that night, the building had been burned to the ground.

Still, we carried on.

Kevin: "That first summer when we had the sacred fire going, there was always ceremonies and teachings going on. I wasn't the only young one; there was a lot of people my own age."

Twelve-year-old Leland George was there a lot. He was Stewart's son, Abraham's grandson. Abraham looked after Leland a lot in that first year while Stewart was in the Maplehurst Correctional Centre.

Marcia: "My mother would do teachings. Traditional songs. She had a hand drum. There were all these sorts of things that pulled people together ... And I remember, you'd see Dudley going down the road there when she was doing some teaching. He was trying to learn the language from Mum."

Marcia shared some of the language she was teaching at school – two high schools in London and an elementary school too. She used a hand puppet she had made herself.

"I called it *Giiwnaadzii Bezhgoogzhiinh*. That means 'Crazy Horse.' And all those kids that came – and there were a lot of them – they all called it that."

Cully: "And we'd have people come in and do ceremonies, and you could just feel at home doing it. Because they took it away from the people a while ago. And then when they did allow them to have pow wows and things again, a lot of them didn't remember, so they didn't do it. It was only the older ones. And you couldn't talk about it openly at the reserve because you had all the Christians there ...

"By then, I had pretty well given up on the church, because I got tired of them tellin' me: 'It's your bed; you gotta lie in it.' So when we moved up here and started doin' ceremonies, it was like: 'This is where I belong!' Everybody's like me.

"That's when it was comin' back for Native people to be themselves more, and that's what I did comin' here. It wasn't really 'til I moved up here that I got more of an education. Like, there was nothing about Indians in the history books – except for way back, and after that they just kinda forgot about us ...

"And I know I have to get much more [education] yet. I missed *many* years of all of those teachings. I can't sit there and story tell. I can only tell about what's happened in my life. But I can't carry on what anybody else's stories were."

Kevin: "A lot of the people I'd never met because they were from everywhere. People had been living all over in the nearby cities and towns, and when word got out, 'We're goin' home,' a lot came home. For me it was exciting to meet all these people and thinking this was goin' to be the start of rebuilding our homeland. Oh, there were arguments. But for the most part, it was great."

Marlin: "There was a lot of sweats; a lot of sweats went on. You just go and, well, you have a sweat to pretty much purify yourself or clear up whatever's bothering you and just get yourself ready for – I don't know; whatever."

Kevin: "First time I did a sweat was at Stoney Point."

Glenn: "It's something, if you go through the thirteen-moon process of doing these things as a sacredness, you'll begin to understand that that wood's going to warm you up half a dozen times before you get in the lodge. You're going to get warmed up from it by gathering the wood, cutting the wood, splitting the wood, carrying the wood. You're going to get warmed up – you're going to sweat long before you get in the lodge ... That's the thing that I kindly learned from my mum and dad. I didn't need nobody from who knows where coming to tell me this is what I should be doing. I'm right in the spot where I'm supposed to be, doing what I'm doing.

"I remember [at Cliff's place] we had a little sweat going there. We had the lodge there one night, and I remember he even moved it up closer toward the barracks, and that was part of the inspiration [that elders like him provided], that we were doing the encroaching. And I thought that was pretty cool, to see old warriors doing that."

A HOLE IN THE HELICOPTER?

Students and professors from Trent University, in Peterborough, showed up with cameras to make a film. People from Fanshawe College in London came out to support us and from different church groups too. And hundreds came from other First Nations, from local reserves like Walpole Island, Chippewas of the Thames, and the Oneida Nation of the Thames; they are part of the Iroquois/Six Nations Confederacy, the Haudenosaunee, and are good allies.

Glenn: "When something happens in Indian Country, they're not going to run and hide. They're going to gather what they can to help their people. That's the way Indians are."

When any of these people arrived, they came first to the sacred fire.

Kevin: "Fire is sacred to the Native people. It's in a lot of our ceremonies. We offer some *semaa* [tobacco] or other medicine ... When tending that fire, being a fire keeper, you're expected to be clean – free from drugs and booze for at least three days prior so you have a clean mind and clean spirit. Dudley was one. He might have been one of the most dedicated ones ...

"We call it a council by having that fire. It's not just living people. You call in all your relations, your spirit animals. The eagle, he's the one who takes our prayers to the Creator, speaks on our behalf ...

"A lot of ceremonies help, I guess, deal with anger. A lot of people were angry. They wanted action to be done. They wanted to do more than just occupy the piece of land ... They wanted to see some recognition from the government."

Cully: "I was sitting by the fire one night, and [a cadet] just kind of came up, right out of the darkness. And he was telling us that the army was telling him not to come over there; that the Natives over there couldn't speak English. And they had a whole bunch of arms and he would never be seen again ... [just] floating in the water somewhere. I told him I was talking in English to him and, 'No, we don't have no arms.' And I told him that they were probably telling them that just to scare them, to stay away from us.

"They used to fly a helicopter over at night, really low and shining lights on people and just making a racket. Right over top of our sacred fire too, knowing that there was ceremonies taking place. They'd bring this thing in at treetop level and just blow stuff everywhere. And then they claim to have gotten shot at."

Rose: "There was all kinds of helicopters. There was police helicopters and there was the army ... continuously, about every two hours. They were annoying because you were just getting to sleep and a helicopter would fly over and wake you up. But I guess that was their intention, to keep us awake and maybe scare us off. And they shone their lights on us; that night wasn't any different."

It was the night they had held a ceremony for Rose's daughter, Marena, who had died in a car accident; a medicine man had come. And then the helicopter flew over, making its terrible noise, stirring up the fire, sending ash all over, and lights blaring into our faces. The next day, suddenly we were swarmed with OPP. The helicopter guys said they had heard a thud when they were flying over us that night, and then they put out this picture showing a hole in the tail section of the helicopter, and they claimed it was from a bullet.

Cully: "I seen the police coming right across the range, toward the road ... like one big wave right across the whole area and then going through the trailers. And if someone wasn't there to open them up, they would just kind of rip them open and go through everything."

Kevin: "They said it [the helicopter] got shot and they used that as an excuse to raid. And they come in, and they took all the paper they could find. Lookin' for weapons, mind. But they took all of our paper," including the band list we had been putting together, by hand; no computers, no copying machines. "It was a community effort; everybody was going back through their family trees. I think it was twenty-two families that was removed in 1942. So that kind of put a stymie into things. And there was minutes from all our meetings; who said what and stuff."

Rose: "They searched the whole camp from the back to the front because they thought somebody shot the helicopter. They started off at the beach and they had dogs and they walked all through the bush and searched. It took them all day. They went through our camp with a fine-tooth comb. And they did find a broken bee-bee gun and a slingshot and a flare gun."

CHAPTER SIX

Peacekeepers
and Nation Builders

Peacekeepers from the Oneida Long House and Oneida Nation of the Thames shared teachings about warrior societies and their traditions. These teachings come out of the Haudenosaunee Constitution, which is more than five hundred years old. It's called *Kayanerenko':wa,* "the Great Law of Peace." The Iroquoian word for "warrior" is *rotiskenhrakete.* In their language, this means: "the one who carries the burden of peace." *Sken* or *skennen* means "peace," and *hrakete* connotes both "burden" and "carrying."[1] Some society members call themselves warriors. Others call themselves peacekeepers.

We decided to set up something like this here, for the young people especially.

Kevin: "We had talked about possibly naming it something different instead of Warrior Society when it was mentioned that a bunch of people seen in the paper [that when] they talk about Warrior Society, they think of Oka and stuff like that where people are masked and armed. And we had had that ceremony where we had buried the hatchet and we were always talking about living in a peaceful manner ...

"We were given a name by Abraham. He said he would think about it for a while, sleep on it, as those older guys usually said – 'Need to sleep on it.'

"He come back. We had another meeting, and he gave us the name of the *Etwaagnikejig.* His definition was 'nation builders,' and that was given to us as young people. That was our duty. We would eventually be building a nation, and that's what we were doing there.

"Our duties were basically to help one another, help the elders, cutting firewood. If we were lucky hunting, we'd share some of the meat, the fishing ... And it also included duties of learning the history and the culture that we were taught at the sacred fire ... and be proud of who we were, where we were." And learning to share the responsibility of leadership.

Glenn: "In our culture we're all leaders ... Not one person has the single role, to make decisions. It's a consensus thing. I've been referred to in the media as a councillor ... that I've been acclaimed [as] leader. I don't know who was acclaiming this; it's not me. To me, in our culture, if you're asked to do those types of things, as a headman, well, you're agreeing to do all those things that involve serving your people within your community ... My uncle [Clifford] was risen up as the headman [elder], and I was the subordinate that would do his legwork, be his eyes, his ears ... That's how it is in our culture ... They need water? You get them water; they need wood, you get them wood."

Marlin: "[Being called an elder] was something that would be earned. They'd have to know a lot of stuff, like about ceremony. They would offer insight into the different ceremonies and stuff that we'd do. They'd open up the meetings with prayers."

But no one in Ottawa would recognize this kind of leadership. They wouldn't even talk to us.

In early August 1993, Kettle and Stony Point band council chief Tom Bressette went to Ottawa to meet with the minister of National Defence, Tom Siddon. He was accompanied and supported by other local and regional chiefs.

Tom: "And we went through the whole scenario of telling him the treaty was set aside ... And we told him we felt that the War Measures Act didn't apply to this land because it was not part of Canada. It was never surrendered to Canada ...

"We went through that whole process with him and basically told him our people wanted that land returned. We explained all the frustration that we encountered previously trying to get in the catering contracts and the attempts to get contracted employment there.

"That was all conveyed to him, and we told him we wanted the government to release that land ... and the people that worked there, it was nothing more than a luxury retirement camp for a lot of the former military officers, and I think I referred him back to a documentary that was put on [the CBC's *The*] *Fifth Estate* ...

"We went into all of those things, told the minister that it appeared to us that this was nothing more than the Cadillac of cadet camps and we never seen no real military usage of the property ... And he basically came back with a response: 'I'm sorry but we still need the land.'"

On August 19, the minister followed up with a letter:

> As I underlined in our meeting, Camp Ipperwash is essential to the Canadian Forces (CF) training programs in the southern Ontario area. The camp is still needed for military purposes and will continue to be needed into the foreseeable future ...
>
> Since you indicated that some of the Band members including some elders do not fully understand why the CF cannot vacate Camp Ipperwash and how the training conducted there fits into the overall government plan, I've asked General Vernon to contact you to offer an information session for your members.

The information session did not go well.

The annual Lieutenant Governor (LG) Day was coming up. This was when the lieutenant governor of Ontario came to inspect the cadets at the end of their summer training. Many of us, particularly women like Marcia and Cully, had worked in the kitchens on that day when they were young, preparing food and cleaning up afterward. So they knew how the day went, what went on. They knew about the parade.

Marcia: "I have this beautiful buckskin outfit that I made; I remember putting that on, because that in itself raises awareness." Cully also wore a traditional outfit that she had made herself.

Cully: "We knew the cadets all marched around the parade square and that the lieutenant governor would be there ... and we took signs that said, 'Welcome to Stoney Point.' And we were dressed in Native attire and carrying our banners and as soon as the parade went by, we joined right in and went right around the parade square with them, right behind them: Welcome to Stoney Point!"

Marcia: "Oh, they were so angry! They were yelling at us: 'This is Camp Ipperwash!'"

Kevin: "The MPs, they tried to take that banner away from my Mum and Cully."

Marcia: "We just rolled it around us. We twirled around and around so it was wrapped around us, from both ends."

Kevin: "There was quite a few demonstrators that had gone in and done different things, holding up signs. [As part of the demonstration] I dropped off what remained of that [burned up] shed. I told them that this is our land, but if they wanted their building, this was what was left of it ... But the MPs were more concerned with taking that sign away from my mum and Cully than with me dropping off that building."

Our little protest got some coverage in the media, which we were happy about. But a few days later an unsigned letter addressed to Kevin Simon made its way to the army camp and even to where he was living, in a cabin some of us had helped him build back in the bush.

Kevin: "It wasn't a very sympathetic letter by any means." In fact, it was three pages of threats and racist hatred. On the last page it said: "You Indian piece of shit, maybe next time the soldiers will lynch you. You Indians are all the same as N–s, fucking scum."

Kevin: "I took it as a threat to me personally, but ... there were numerous people that would stop along the highway as we were camped out [there], just pull over to the side of the road and yell out whatever came to their mind, I guess. Usually along the same lines as that letter."

MARCH TO OTTAWA

Then it was September. The kids were back in school. Not as many supporters were coming around. The days were getting shorter; the nights were getting colder. A lot of people were getting fed up because nothing was happening. So we thought, if they won't come to us, we should go to them. We would walk there too; this way, many of us could go. We actually got the idea from someone in Kitchener-Waterloo who had decided to do a march for us himself. He didn't get very far, and we never did find out what happened to any of the money that he raised. We decided that we'd do our own march to Canada's capital city. We would walk the whole seven hundred kilometres – take our case there directly. Speak for ourselves, not through lawyers, not relying on the chief and band council at Kettle Point. And raise awareness. There was about thirty of us, the elders driving but the younger ones walking.

Glenn: "We were walking for home. The Stoney Point Long Walk for Home is what it was called. [We weren't] going there to place threats or anything. It was to try, I guess, to put a face on those people that were making the decision, who was keeping the land from the people."

Rose: "We had to have places to stay at night and Pearl and I kind of went ahead and I asked for places to stay. I think it was the OAC [Ontario Agricultural College in Guelph], their picnic grounds, they let us stay for nothing.

"And some people heard of us coming, and they would invite us to their homes. And we were well received all along, and the boys that walked all the way – Glenn, and that Danny [Martin Kewageshig, Pearl George's nephew]," plus Rose's own son Bert, "they had blisters galore.

"We had a lot of pamphlets that were about Stoney Point and about our plight ... to bring awareness to the people, to the non-Native people and also to the Native people, because we went through all the reserves. We took Number 7 all the way to Ottawa; I think we jogged off a bit in Toronto there. [It was just] we would like if they would support us in getting our land back."

Glenn: "My uncle Cliff was there, and he never made nothing about needing a room. He slept in his little pony car. And that was the thing, you know. When you're going to do these things, it's nice to have those old people as your witness ... and it helped to bring out an understanding with other people. Not every community had people there to greet us ... We weren't looking for that; we were trying just to raise awareness.

"But we did have where people come out, and they had some of their reporters. They had gifts; some had food. You know, they asked, can we share a meal with you? I remember we were just outside of Toronto and the Mennonite Central Committee, they put us up in a summer camp ... and things just worked out."

Rose: "And the reserves, we stayed there maybe two days because they would raise money for us to carry on. And they would have a feast for us, have a blanket dance. And we had some pretty good places in the white communities too. I know one place, there was like a big dance floor. They had a real good meal there."

Glenn: "We stayed at Tyendinaga [reserve];[2] we got Kentucky Fried Chicken two nights in a row. Golden Lake [reserve]; they put us up in a barn. Thirteen different kinds of corn they plant there ...

"Visitors all along there, eh? Different tribes, they all come out; come along to visit. Different ones would do ceremonies. They would have women there; they'd sing songs for four or five hours straight. And there were healing ceremonies for people with sore feet. They'd pull right up and there'd be big fuckin' vats of cedar all boiled up. You'd put your feet right in there. They'd smudge you down. They'd make you drink a whole jar of cedar tea, and you're all doctored up ...

"When you do things in ceremony, they fall together perfect. I might limp around today – I can still feel my knee aching from walking on the lopsided shoulder of the road. But I look at it as, to me, that's nobody else's business but my own."

Janet: "I walked some; just a little bit." Mostly, she drove her car, carrying things like the pamphlets and souvenir-message hats that Rose Manning had made. She and Rose gave these out and also used them to raise a bit of money. She, her mother, Pearl, and Rose Manning also lined up food and places to sleep along the way.

"The people that were on the walk, they were hungry and in need of smokes. And all along, people would donate cans and cans of food. And people were donating money. People were handing us cheques."

At an event organized by a Mennonite Church in Kitchener, one of the marchers, Albert Jamieson, told a local newspaper reporter: "The support is overwhelming and that reinforces the fact that we are right!"[3]

It was different, though, when we arrived on Parliament Hill in Ottawa.

Janet: "It was lunchbag letdown. We got there to say something, but it was 'So what? We made it here and there's nothing.' There was somebody [who came out to speak with us]. But it wasn't somebody you'd call important."

Rose: "There was nothing. We had a big party when we arrived – right on Parliament Hill. A lot of picture taking, but there was no media. There was no one" there to receive us, talk to us, listen to us. "I guess they all knew we were coming so they all went and barricaded themselves somewhere. But we never seen them. We looked around, but [the building] was so high."

Glenn: "I'd never been there before myself, until that day. I remember it looked so ... I seen this fountain, and there was flames coming out of it and it kind of, 'Holy, look at that; it's magic!'

"And I was walking up the stairs and we had our Aazhoodena flags and stuff and the eagle staff and a couple of pipes that travelled with us.

"I remember we got up close and you look up and you see these things poking out the corners of the building [with] these horns and big fangs and, 'What the heck is that?'

"We walked all the way here to – and you look up and, they looked like those gargoyle things. I don't know what they are. They looked kind of scary, eh? And you kind of question, 'Was I at the right place or not?'

"Nobody from within that building come out [to meet with us]."

No senior government official, no one from a minister's office, none of the cabinet ministers responsible for holding up our lives. Basically, nobody.

Rose: "We took Bert's van up and it was right full of stuff – feathers and blankets and donations. So we touched the hearts of some people. It wasn't futile. And even, you know, getting up and going there and getting along. Because every morning we would get up, and first thing we done was greet each other, and we smoked a pipe, and we drank the water and ate the berries. Every single day, even the Christians. So this is what we done. We had closer contact with each other, and we prayed every morning before we ate. A lot of people, if they weren't dressed, they just got up and ran for the sunrise service."

Kevin: "When the walk to Ottawa was taking place, [Dudley] had been basically the only one that stayed back. I was in London at the time, and I come back, and I realized that the base was pretty well abandoned except for Dudley. He was still there tending that fire. So I stayed and helped, too.

"I was always glad to see him; he was a joker. I remember when I attended kindergarten in Kettle Point, he was taking an upgrading course at the same time – same building. I remember he started a snowball fight with the kids; received the worst end of it, but he was that type of person. He remembered all the kids' names; always knew what they were up to ... I remember my grandparents received a letter from him when he was spending time in – I believe it was Guelph; he was locked up.[4] And my brother was one of those ones that would take him fishing. I was quite a bit younger, so I wasn't allowed."

Then winter set in, and not all of us could stay in our little trailers and tents on the land. But Clifford and Dudley did. They stayed there the whole winter – with no electricity, no running water, no indoor toilet. They kept the fire going in their wood stoves. They had kerosene lamps and candles. Clifford passed the time carving turtles and other creatures out of wood and selling them. He even sold one to an OPP officer.

Gina: "I remember playing euchre with Dudley in the middle of the night, by candlelight, on New Year's Eve when he was in that trailer – and peeing in the snow outside!"

Marcia: "We'd heard rumours that some of the local people around were taking bets as to how long our people would stay there, once the cold weather set in, because they were pretty makeshift conditions they were living in. It was a record cold winter as well. And they made it through.

"So we planned to have a feast to honour them, and it was Clifford's birthday, and Dudley's [close in date] too. And the Stoney Point women, the *Aazhoodena-kwe,* as we called ourselves, planned this celebration and decided upon a program. I was selected to do the tribute to Dudley, and Clifford's sister Bernice was to do the one for Clifford. I had banners done up in Ojibwe, *Mno-dbishkaa Giizhgad,* 'happy birthday' Dudley, and he actually took those home with him and put them up in his trailer.

"In this tribute, I started off: On March the 7th, 1957, a little brown baby boy ... was born in Sarnia ... and he hated Sundays because he had to join them in the Port Huron Church ... In the early 1970s, Dudley joined the Banana Splits Club. Dudley also wrote into the *National Inquirer* after spotting a TV blooper, winning for himself a blooper T-shirt and a special certificate. But all was not happy ... Dudley also spent some time in Guelph but gained valuable experience by sitting on the Native Sons executive committee and, at the same time, his older brother Pierre was in Birch, and they corresponded with each other ... And about this time, Dudley's younger brother Peter passed away. Then, in 1986, our Grandma Laura went on to the next life and Dudley's father also joined her ...

"In May 1993 ... finally some roots, finally a community and finally a home ...

"And in closing, we give thanks to *Gzhe-mnidoo* [the Creator] for you, for making it through ... May you continue to work as an Etwaagnikejig [a nation builder] for Stoney Point."

CHAPTER SEVEN

Taking the Barracks

1994–September 4, 1995

The government in Ottawa had cut funding for the cadet training camp in 1994, and DND was down to just a few people around to keep the army base running. The Ontario minister for Native Affairs wrote to his federal counterpart urging the government to return our land. But as usual, nothing was happening that we could see.

The days were getting shorter again. Winter would be coming on soon, and we knew how cold it gets in the trailers. For the younger ones, this meant hauling more trees out of the bush and sawing them up, chopping and stacking the wood not just for ourselves, but for the elders as well. And our elders were getting older. Abe had an oxygen tank now; he also had congestive heart failure. And yet over there, most of the barracks in the built-up area were empty.

One of Abe's grandsons, Nicholas Cottrelle, told his mother: "Pretty soon Grandpa's not going to be here ... All they do is talk, talk, talk. We're tired of hearing talk. We're just going to take some action and that's all there is to it."[1]

Maynard got himself elected onto the Kettle and Stony Point band council and took a resolution to hold a separation referendum to the council. If it passed, we would finally be in a position to negotiate directly with the federal government for the return of our land.

But the Kettle and Stony Point council decided not to authorize a referendum vote. Maynard resigned his seat on the band council. But of course that didn't make any difference.

There were fewer supporters coming to Stoney Point. The sacred fire was no longer kept lit.

Kevin: "There was people that had come down here; non-Native supporters [bringing pizzas and other gifts]. I remember one person in particular came around, maybe a year later. Dudley was asking how come they hadn't been around in such a long time. They related a story to us about being raided, their house being raided, their greenhouse being rummaged through, their tomato plants being up-rooted and stuff. My belief was, and their belief as well, was that there was a connection [to] their support of what we were doing here in Stoney."

Some of the people who came, media especially, would ask us how long we planned to keep up the occupation, the protest. They didn't understand. This wasn't some short demonstration type of occupation where after it's done, you go back home. We *were* back home, along with our kids and our grandkids. We were picking up the threads of what our people had to leave behind in 1942. We were trying to stitch them back together, making a shared life for everyone again here at Aazhoodena. We weren't asking permission anymore either. We were doing it. We had come back to the land the Creator gave to our ancestors to look after, something that the Treaty of Niagara, and our understanding of it in the two-row wampum belt, plus the Huron Tract Treaty, respected. We were living our treaty rights – our collective treaty rights – and our responsibilities too. We wanted the government in Ottawa to respect this, to recognize this and act. But they would not. (We found out later that the government told Tom Bressette that they would not get on with negotiating for the return of our land "until the current trespass at Camp Ipperwash ends." This was in a letter from the minister of National Defence in August 1993.)

Things were getting worse between us and the people at the army base too. They were taunting us more with things like "You forgot to pay your taxes." And they were sneaking into our area at night, slashing tents, stealing our flags. There were other incidents: The tires of Marlin's car were slashed. Not just punctured; slashed so they were wrecked. They couldn't be used anymore. Then the military put up barriers across the road at a bridge that we used to cross the creek. No lights, no warning sign. By now, Glenn had replaced Carl as our Stoney Point chief.

Glenn: "I work in the construction business, and I know: You've got to have signs. You've got to have lights. And they didn't have nothing ... And I went there and wrapped the chain around and just yanked them out [with the tractor] and drove away with them; that's all I did. And that's when the military guys come out. Like, I didn't go there to look for a confrontation. I just went there to open up the road. And my statement to them [was]: 'This is my land, and you're trespassing on my land, and you're also trying to block off roads on my land ...' And I got a criminal record now because of this."

That happened near the end of June 1995, and by then we were fed up. We wanted the army gone. More people talked about moving up there, taking over the barracks, hoping the elders would agree. Maybe it might put more pressure on the government.

Janet: "Everybody – all the people from in the camp – said: 'Let's have a meeting down at the lake, along the beach.' And, 'We're gonna go in and take the barracks.'"

Rose: "Actually, we were quite happy to be where we were [in our campers and makeshift cabins down by the ranges]. And it was a Friday evening, we were having a picnic of sorts in front of Pearl George's cabin in the place where the school used to be, and the church. So we were having this picnic, and this media person from the *Globe and Mail* showed up. He said, 'I'm from the *Globe and Mail*,' and he thought we should give him a story. Well, I wouldn't give him a story. We were just having a great time, and he came along, and so I kind of maybe said some things I shouldn't have said, like 'Why should I?' He said, 'I'm from the *Globe and Mail*,' and I said, 'So?'

"So he got upset too. When I got upset, I made him upset too. And he said, 'So, what are you going to do come Monday when the special police move in?' And I said, 'Oh, the special police are moving in?' He said, 'Yes they are, and what are you going to do then?' I said, 'Oh well, we'll deal with it when Monday comes, I guess.' And I said, 'Well, we'll see you.' And he left.[2] And as soon as he left, we said, well, I guess we'll have to go in sooner than we had expected to go in. We'll have to go in on Saturday. We'll go in at 12:30 because I have to do my yard sale-ing first. I have a booth at the flea market; that's the way I was helping with things I was doing."

Barracks Takeover: July 29, 1995

Rose: "It was that quick. One minute we were laughing and carefree and everything. The next minute we were planning to go into the built-up area. I said, 'We'll go in at 12:30 because everybody will have had their lunch, and they won't even expect us' ... And we went to the beach and met there. We just kind of had a quick plan there as to who was going in the cars, and who was going to take the back, and who was going to take the side.

"And the bus went in on the side, and it was full of children and a lot of my grandchildren."

Warren George's son Harley was driving. He lived in Sarnia, went to school there. He was fifteen and in Grade 8. He'd been coming around a lot on the weekends, and he had fixed up a place to sleep in the bus and kind of appointed himself as the one to take care of it. He had taught himself how to drive it, too; a lot of our young people had. And he'd driven it a half dozen or so times before that day, on the gravel roads through the bush here at Stoney Point.

Clifford: "We were there long enough, so – so, we decided that it's time; time we moved on a little further ... We just pulled in [into the area where the base headquarters and parade grounds were] with a bus and told them that we're taking over the camp now."

Rose: "Our car went in first – I know it did because we were watching that bus because it had my grandchildren in it. And when we stopped, I lifted the gate and Bruce [Manning] and Maynard – he must have jumped out, and they went in together to serve the eviction notice."

Marlin: "My point of entry was at the road they called the Strand; there was a barrier right around there. Just a sawhorse kind of thing. And barbed wire all across ... and spiked bars that were all along the way [in the grass] there. If anybody wanted to drive around it, they would get their tires flattened. My job was to go and gather up those things and throw them in the trunk or throw them off in the bushes somewhere ... And then we just went for a quick ride around, around the parade square."

Marcia: "I came in from the range from our grandparents' estate. I drove eastward into the barracks from there, as far as I could go. They had barricades set up with those tire slashers and things so you couldn't drive over them.

"Others came in from the inland lakes there, driving the school bus. There was a gate there; they drove right through it. That ole school bus; it could do a lot of stuff."

Janet: "I was coming in from the beach, in my truck. And when I came in, I went circling around the parade square. I was circling around there with the truck.

"And Glenn, he came through the bush with a tractor. And Bruce Manning and Maynard were at the gate and they were serving papers to those guys. They said: 'We are taking over now. You have to get out. Get out now. Leave everything. Drop everything. Get out! We're taking over the barracks.'"

Marcia: "So I went over there, and I told them, 'I want you boys out of here.' And to the female officers, I told them: 'I want you girls out of here as well. This is our territory.' Just said it calmly and told them what I wanted ... But some of them, when they saw me coming, they would run and hide behind the trucks and things, and I was just an old woman going to town with my wish list.

"But they made us sound like we were a bunch of vicious warriors! If they just knew that we were a bunch of teenagers, plus there's me and my mum, old grey-haired widows. Same with ole Pearl."

Cully: "First thing I did, I did circles around the parade square, because you were never allowed to go on the parade square before ... The guys would screech and burn rubber, but I didn't know how to do that, so I just went in circles."

Rose: "I was at the main gate still, but the rest of the people went in and then Nellie Rogers drove back. She said, 'Rose, they're fighting with our kids.' They went right after that bus. So I jumped in with her."

Harley was driving the bus around and around the parade square with a bunch of MPs on his tail in their jeeps. He wasn't going fast, but he wasn't stopping either. He was afraid to; afraid he'd get arrested. So he kept driving, doing kind of figure eights around the big trailer trucks they had in there for loading up stuff from the camp. And then he drove up to the drill hall, rec hall, right up to the double doors, and started pushing on them. But they wouldn't open. So he put the bus in reverse so he could turn around and keep going another way. But one of MPs had driven his jeep right in behind the bus and parked it sideways. Harley backed up anyway, pushing the jeep back so he could get enough space to make the turn. But then the bus door popped open, and one of the MPs jumped up on the step with a can of pepper spray.

Rose: "By the time I got there it was pretty well kind of over with. And I seen those kids. They were all pepper sprayed. And there was a big hullabaloo about getting the kids out. Somebody opened the back door to get the children out. And the guy who was driving [Harley], he was all pepper sprayed, and I think somebody drove him to the beach real quick" because he had been sprayed right in the face; one eye got it pretty bad.

"And my grandchild got pepper sprayed too, and he was just a little fellow [age six] at the time. And he said: 'Well I got sprayed accidentally.'"

And then we carried on with what we were doing.

Cully: "We went in the kitchens first. The Savoy was completely equipped; that was the only kitchen that was open to feed the guys still here."

Gina: "It was like Christmas; everybody grab a building. Some were fully equipped too."

Marlin: "And hot showers!"

Janet: "I was just looking around and then my cousin Brenda Oliver – she's Brenda George now – she says: 'Come on, Jan. Everbody's gettin' them places.'"

Marcia: "My mum and I stayed in the old chapel. It was unheated, which is probably why nobody was fighting over that!"

They left the confessional in the back corner. They took out the benches and other church things and ended up laying down lines for quilting work on the floor. Marcia installed a wood stove in the back where the chaplain's quarters had been; she and Melva settled in nicely.

But all that came later. On the day we took over the barracks, somebody had spotted a couple of OPP cruisers come in, and word went around that they were going to treat what Harley did as a crime; they were sending in people to investigate. More and more of us drifted back to the parade square to find out what was happening. There was a new guy in charge: Captain William Douglas (Doug) Smith. He had settled things down in the parade square earlier; told his MPs to back off and go about their regular business. We sent him a message that we wanted the OPP to stop investigating. Later, a couple of guys associated with the Oneida Long House and the Oneida Nation of the Thames showed up. Peacekeepers. One was Bob Antone. A few of us knew him and respected him. He was involved in a lot of conflict mediation work; he was even at Oka. That evening, he came over and talked with us, told us he would do what he could. We waited. It got dark. And suddenly the army people were packing up their stuff and leaving.

Rose: "They just handed over the keys. They said we have to keep up the buildings, and they would be leaving."

Clifford: "They left voluntarily, no problems, no nothing. They even left us a whole kitchen. Of course we had to ask them, 'Jeez, at least leave us that.'"

Rose: "And that kitchen was the only one that was really in use. And the freezers, they were right full of meat and chicken and fish and whatever you want. Steaks. Oh, those guys ate a lot of it. For the first time we had a gourmet meal – that same evening."

Marlin couldn't sleep that night, he was so excited: "It was just, it seemed like [we] finally got the land back from the military. It seemed like something that was way distant, like it never seemed like [we] were going to get the land back. And then, finally, it just seemed like we had the land back!"

Chief Tom Bressette was shocked: "The army abandoned their outpost! They took the flag with them, and they ran down the road. That's what they did ... And our people went in and took the land back. That's what should have happened naturally."

He convened a council meeting. This was followed, on August 2, by a press release: "People attending the meeting stated that they want to work with the Band members occupying the Stoney Point land to reunify the community torn apart by the illegal appropriation and continued use by the Military of half our land base." The release went on to say: "Non-band members in occupation of Camp Ipperwash should be asked to leave."

These were all the people from other reserves who had come out to support us when no one else did, including the Oneida peacekeepers and others from the Oneida Nation of the Thames. We found out later that not everyone had agreed with this. Bonnie (Bressette) was one. We also learned that Tom had taken off on holidays the next day, but that he'd also received a phone call from the national chief of the Assembly of First Nations, Ovide Mercredi, offering to mediate the differences between us and the band council at Kettle Point. Tom turned down his offer.

But Tom did fly to Ottawa later: "I was told to go down there and put things on the table, which I did. And I met Maynard, who claimed he was meeting with the minister ... The minister never knew whether

I had anybody behind me ... I wanted to talk about the land for everybody. I was an elected chief sent by this community ... and the [people in the] minister's office were laughing, 'Ha-ha-ha. I dunno; maybe he's gonna meet with that fella sitting over there on a bench with a bag and a bottle.'

"They would refuse to meet with me. I was met by a deputy or an ADM or somebody else down the chain; never the minister.

"They were all very angry at the council down here for not supporting them [meaning us, Stoney Pointers]. And we [the chief and band council] said, 'It would have been better if you had come and notified [us] that you were going to do this on behalf of the community instead of just a mob of you goin' in there ... Some people have an agenda for the people, and that's what my agenda was: for this community."

Bernard George watched all this from two sides: from his seat on the band council and from what he had seen and heard when he spent time camping and visiting with us here at Stoney Point.

Bernard: "There was a communications gap. I didn't like to see it, but it happened."

Stewart George moved into one of the barracks: "It was around the middle of August, 'cause the kids weren't going to school yet ... My son [Leland] wanted to go live up there and help the cause. And, well, that's where we're from ...

"[Dudley] watched Leland while I'd go to work in Kettle Point, and Leland [was] more or less having fun, being chauffeur for Dudley, driving Dudley around. He had a chauffeur cap and all that, and people were laughing, telling me how Dudley was babysitting. I don't know who was watching who.

"He [Leland] was around twelve or thirteen. Dudley showed him how [to drive]." But only around this little piece of our territory with the army's barbed-wire fence around it.

There were lots of cars people only drove on the base. They were usually big, old vehicles from the '60s or even before. You could buy these for a hundred dollars or less. No insurance, no licence. Duct tape keeping side mirrors from falling off. Vapour barrier in side and back windows.

Kevin: "They're rez cars; rez bombs, some people call them."

Gina: "With baloney-skin tires" – worn down so much there was often no tread left at all.

Leland: "My dad was doing construction work in Kettle Point so I would stay with Dudley and, like, he taught me to drive and stuff. He used to get me to wear a hat and drive him around ... I didn't consider it a game. I thought it was fun though."

Dudley and Robert Isaac, who was a friend of Cully's, painted a big "OPP Who" sign on the side of the car that Robert drove around a lot. It was a taunt at the OPP, a sort of "Who are you?"

Gina: "I was excited by the full-on kitchen, because back in the day they were feeding hundreds of people three times a day. So once we took back that, I immediately fell into that role – the cook crew. And other crews, like with "Worm" [Stewart] and Glenn, were on water works. And we had checkpoints around." Our peacekeepers had been patrolling the perimeter of the territory we had first claimed down by the ranges. Now they had expanded, patrolling the whole base like the MP, the military police, had done.

"That was one of my jobs as well: to make sure the guys had breakfast, lunch, and supper. And some other women came from the US to help, and it was 'so and so's got some space in their barrack, put em up there.'

"I loved that – the sharing. That was the best part."

Stewart: "Everybody was happy because the army was gone and people would, you know, go and visit here and go and visit over there. There was just a feeling ... I don't know how to describe it, but everybody seemed pretty happy anyway."

Clifford was one of the ones who stayed living back by the bush where many of our old homesteads used to be.

Clifford: "I said, no way I'm gonna move into them [barracks]. I lived in them too long."

Janet: "I used to go there, take a loaf of bread and a pound of butter. I knew he had a woodstove. So I'd go down there. 'Hey, Cliff, you got any tea?'

"'Yeah, come on in.' And he'd be sittin' there. 'Hey Cliff, I brought some bread and butter. Let's have some toast.'

"'All right!'

"I really enjoyed that."

Abe originally settled into a room with a bed at the back of the maintenance garage. But someone noticed the sergeant major's house was empty; Abe might be more comfortable there.

Joy (his daughter): "I painted all over that house before he moved in. Almost before; he couldn't wait. Because he wanted to come home," and this felt like he was fully home, finally; having a real roof over his head. "And Mum [still living at Kettle Point], there were people pulling pranks on her. Somebody threw a bag of rotten fish guts in her driveway. It had just millions of maggots in it. And then one day somebody called me and said: 'your mum wants you to come down; her phone's not workin.' And I called, and they come in and looked at it, and the guy come in and said: 'the wire outside has been cut with one of these – wire cutters.'

"She said: 'I wanna move up there with your dad.'"

MOVING INTO IPPERWASH PARK

There had been talk of taking over the park [Ipperwash Provincial Park] as far back as May 1993. Maynard T. George had even drawn up a notice advising the person receiving it "not to resist or willingly obstruct the legal seizure and repossession of the identified lands" as a lawful part of the Stoney Point Reserve. It was signed by Carl George, who was our first chief, along with a number of our councillors, including Rose Manning, Janet Cloud, and Clifford George. Maynard got the bailiff, Scott Ewart, to serve this notice to the park's superintendent, Les Kobayashi, to make it official. We found out later that he ended up serving it on one of the summer employees when he couldn't find Kobayashi. We had also talked to Kobayashi about us co-managing the park with them, the people at the Ministry of Natural Resources, and our people putting on some programs to educate the public.

It wasn't just that the land had been so-called sold but mostly swindled away from us back in the 1920s when the treaty had promised us the exclusive use and enjoyment of all the land set aside as our reserve. It was the burial grounds that were in there too.

Rose: "My father, he was the chief and a councillor there and continued to be a councillor in Kettle Point. And when I was looking in the archives, I recall seeing my dad's name in several places, and he was saying: 'We have to put a fence around those burial grounds.' And I remember him talking about them too. He seemed to know exactly where the burial ground was because he wanted it fenced-in separate from the park because they were desecrating that burial ground when they camped right there after the park was established there.

"They said there were some people [buried] that were facing west ... and they buried them with all what they needed for their travel ...

That was the people that were travelling through, because we had our own burial ground. This was supposed to be the visitors that would stop in. They would stop in for flint – trade for flint or whatever," and healing.

On the day the bailiff went in (May 18), Maynard led a few of us in too, to do a ceremony, hand out pamphlets, raise awareness. Some of this came to light during the Ipperwash Inquiry. There were notes from phone calls Kobayashi had had with Chief Tom Bressette at the time.

Tom Bressette: "I told him basically, I felt, you know, that trespass charges should be laid against him and leave it up to the appropriate authorities ... I told him, get the OPP to charge him. That's what I told him."

Kevin: "It had been made clear before, when we'd taken over the army base, that we weren't going to ... that our people would be staying within those boundaries ... the lands that were taken in 1942."

Still, the idea of taking back the part of the reserve that had been turned into the provincial park had never gone away completely.

Marlin: "It was kind of something everybody sat around talking about, like, for a few years. Over the course of the few years that we were camped out in the military base there, it kind of come out that, yeah, there was a burial ground inside there and it was supposed to be set aside and marked, and it wasn't.

"And Dudley knew that [that this had been his great-grandfather Albert George's homestead]. That was one of the biggest things – that the beach end was all sold. And it was questionable how they did that because the Indian agent was the same guy who looked after land and real estate, and a few other hats that he wore."

Marcia: "There were only a few burials [of our people] there. But these were our close relatives: people like Kamaanii – Albert George."

J.R.: "It was something Dudley was often talking about, because of the burial grounds in there. He didn't know exactly where, but he didn't want a bunch of campers partying around on those graves ... The idea was to try to get it back for the Stoney Point people and draw some media attention to ourselves; we weren't getting enough media attention [at the army camp]."

Plus, two or three of us might have yelled some things at the army when they were leaving that night at the end of July. Things like "The park is next!" and "We're taking over the park next!" It kind of set us on that path.

Marlin: "I don't know if there was a big plan. It was like, 'this is ours too, and we're gonna have it.'"

Gina: "We were waiting for the [park's] season to be done. We didn't want to disrupt their money-making thing."

Marcia: "I didn't want them to go in there because we were still helter-skelter. [Clifford George and Dudley were still back at the ranges while others were still moving into deserted barracks.] It was such chaos then. We weren't settled ... People were pulled in different directions ... Anyways, they still decided that they were going to do that, so I went along with it."

Clifford: "I wasn't in on the discussion with whomever were going to take the park over ... I wasn't opposed to it ... It was the wrong time ... And, well, I was probably peeved because they didn't consult with me. After all, I'm the elder here."

Marlin: "And we'd been keepin' an eye out and they were getting ready to close it off and shut it down for the winter. And they had these cement blocks that were blockin' the gate, and we noticed them movin' those things out of the way. And that's where we ended up goin' in."

Gina: "I wasn't part of the 'Alright, we're gonna head down there right now.' But I went down there probably hours after that happened."

Marlin: "It wasn't like a regular, drawn out meeting. It was just – people were sitting around, having coffee at the [mess hall, barracks area] kitchen one day and somebody says, 'Well, park's closing down. Are we going to go in there or not?'

"It was just a quick little meeting, and everybody seemed all for it. Everybody said, 'yeah, sure.'"

Janet: "And there's Maynard typing away again. 'It states this and this and this, and that's why we're gonna take it.' And Maynard had these papers to give them: if the police come along, you've got something to hand them."

Marlene Cloud's son, Mike, had started living at the base by then too.

Mike: "I remember Glenny was telling me that they – that Les [Kobayashi] give him the keys. They were, like, negotiating with them guys. They were told ahead of time that they were going to take back the heart of Stoney Point because of the burial grounds, after all the campers were gone."

At 7:30 p.m. on September 4, after the last of the campers had left and the park had closed for the season, Marlin grabbed some bolt cutters and headed down the inside (gravel) road toward the beach.

"And my uncle Glenn come up driving a big ole farm tractor, and we opened up the gate ... The bolt cutters kept slipping off. So I handed my cousin the bolt cutters, and I grabbed that chain and held it so he could snap it off."

Park officials were on the other side. One of them handed over keys for the two buildings before leaving. Then everyone explored around, figuring out which key opened which door. And then an alarm went off.

Marlin: "I was in one of the buildings and the phone rang, and he gave us a code to punch into the alarm system so that it would shut the alarms off."

Someone lit a fire. There was a smudging ceremony and tobacco.

Stewart: "The people were able to take care of them [the people who had been buried in that place] and offer them tobacco ... I offered tobacco into the fire."

Marlin: "Everybody was excited and kind of happy ... Nobody wanted to be seen as a leader of the occupation – for fear of being targeted, for arrest or other things ... Everybody was a leader.

"We didn't really think nothing was going to happen because it was closed down for the year, and there wasn't no possibility of altercation between campers or anything like that."

Only a few stayed down there for the night; mostly young people who were friends with Dudley. James Thomas (J.T.) Cousins was one of them; he was fourteen. He lived in Sarnia with his mother, Marianne, and his stepfather, Anthony Kenneth George. His father was Kenneth Shawkence. J.T. had been friends with Dudley since he was a little kid and had stayed with him until Dudley found him a barracks where he could sleep.

J.T.: "We sat around the fire telling stories, smoking cigarettes."

Some OPP showed up, along with someone with the parks authority. They wanted to serve a trespass notice. We told them we don't do business at night; it was past eleven by then. There was some yelling. One of the teenagers threw a firecracker at the OPP,[3] and they left.

We had a sunrise ceremony the next morning.

CHAPTER EIGHT

September 5–6, 1995, Project Maple

When some of us – the children and grandchildren of long-time Stoney Point families – walked and drove onto the part of our homeland that had been turned into a provincial park, the OPP were ready. Even waiting. It turns out they'd been preparing, too. They'd installed video surveillance cameras at the park kiosk and maintenance building. And they had had four undercover OPP officers in the park for the month of August, disguised as campers. At least one family camping nearby regularly brought them coffee and muffins for breakfast.[1]

The OPP also had a plan. It was called Project Maple. OPP Inspector John Carson was already the incident commander on the case and even had a date marked on his calendar. Glenn George and Bert Manning, who had been on the march to Ottawa together, had informed the OPP that they would be claiming the provincial park after the Labour Day weekend. Carson had already requested clarification that the province held clear title to the land.

In fact, Carson had been involved since May of 1993, when he was a staff sergeant running the OPP detachment in Forest. On May 6, Carl George had paid him a visit as chief of the Stoney Point council, bringing him a copy of the notice we had issued that morning when entering the army base. Shortly after filing a report of this to his superiors, Carson was promoted to inspector and appointed incident commander for Ipperwash. The next day, Detective Sergeant Mark Wright called the Forest detachment and offered to work on any criminal investigations that might arise in the Ipperwash area – he became Carson's second-in-command. The following day, May 21, Carson convened a meeting at OPP headquarters in London (Ontario). He had been researching the history of the 1942 takeover of Stoney Point and been briefed on legal issues including "the colour of right," a civil right that can be used as a defence for people who might be committing a criminal offence, such as trespassing. At the meeting, Carson presented an "OPP Operational Plan" that included, as its guiding principle: "We will essentially act in a facilitating role ensuring that all parties are permitted to execute their respective rights."

Late on the night of August 23, 1993, Carson was advised that two OPP officers had observed a military helicopter flying over the Ipperwash base and also what they believed to be rifle fire coming from the ranges area. He was later advised that a military helicopter had taken a bullet in the tail section. He immediately directed the base to be secured as a crime scene and arranged for a thorough criminal investigation, sending in an Emergency Response Team for the work the next morning with orders to stay all day if necessary to complete the search.

As time went on, there was ongoing confusion over who was responsible for what. The local cottagers (along the shores of Lake Huron, between Kettle Point and Stoney Point in particular) frequently lodged complaints about us. The OPP spent time in the spring and summer of 1994 developing and clarifying policies around this. Staff Sergeant Wade Lacroix issued a memo to all area officers, stating:

> It is imperative that the Ontario Provincial Police be seen by all parties as neutral in this ongoing land dispute. Accordingly, it should not be the practice of officers to take coffee breaks and other extended visits at the military base ... In the event of a MAJOR OCCURRENCE such as the Attempted Murder of the military helicopter crew last summer, the ability of investigators to work effectively is dependent upon all involved parties recognizing the Ontario Provincial Police as a neutral law enforcement agency.

Detective Sergeant Wright also issued a memo, especially directed toward policing in the cottage area, pointing out as Item #2: "The Regional Crown and our Legal Branch have explained that because of the impending legal battle over final ownership of the land [at West Ipperwash Beach] the natives now enjoy what is called 'COLOUR

OF RIGHT.'" He went on to say: "Remember, we are a neutral entity. We will take enforcement action against ANYONE who breaks the law, regardless of race."

Sometime in 1994, the military set up Operation Maple, a special security operation, at Ipperwash, with Captain Allan Percy Howse posted to the base as its commanding officer. Its job was to ensure the safe removal of military assets from the base now that the cadet training camp had been terminated. It was Howse who set up the barricade on the bridge across the creek in the ranges area on the evening of June 27, 1995. When Glenn George, then acting chief of the Stoney Point council, tore it down and challenged Captain Howse to get off our land, the incident was reported to the OPP and charges laid. Glenn pled guilty and was convicted of mischief under five thousand dollars, two counts of assault, and uttering death threats. He was given a suspended sentence and put on probation for fifteen months.

Meanwhile, Howse was reassigned to administrative duties and Captain Doug Smith came in as commanding officer. In one of his first actions, he reached out to Bob Antone and Bruce Elijah, both with the Oneida First Nation and associated with the Oneida Long House of peacekeepers and highly regarded as First Nations negotiators. Like Antone, Elijah had been involved in trying to turn conflict toward peace at Oka. He was also at Wounded Knee and Akwesasne in the 1970s. Smith arranged for them to provide some cross-cultural training for the army personnel at Ipperwash, which they did sometime in mid-July. He also got them to help set up some talks with us Stoney Pointers and started planning for a meeting to talk about cleaning up the base and laying the groundwork for the land to be returned. The meeting was scheduled for August 26 and was supposed to include all the different parties, including the Kettle and Stony Point band council chief. Tom Bressette did not support it, and despite efforts by Elijah and Antone, would not commit to attend. The meeting ended up being cancelled.

On the afternoon of July 29, after we came to take over the barracks, Smith contacted Antone and Elijah and asked them to come back. Meanwhile, a call had gone out to the Forest OPP detachment, and Carson drove out with Wright. He advised Captain Smith to tell us that we were trespassing and, later, that the OPP would be investigating the incident with the bus bashing into the jeep, sending a photographer to record the damage and treating it as "an overt criminal act." When Antone arrived that evening, after he talked to those of us standing around in the parade square, he told Smith that he had a choice: to force us out and risk violence or to leave quietly. In his testimony to the Ipperwash Inquiry, he said that he had advised leaving, saying: "They already said they were going to give it [the land] back. Well, why don't you leave? Why start a big fight here? People are just going to get hurt. What are you losing? You got all your assets loaded up."[2]

The peacekeepers stayed on for a couple of days, and Smith returned to show the people how to operate the hydro and the water systems. He also became the military's liaison with us.

On July 30, Carson met with Lieutenant Colonel Sweeny at the Forest Golf and Country Hotel. Colonel Sweeny made it clear that DND had not surrendered control of the land where Camp Ipperwash was located. They had only left for safety reasons. There were other meetings that day, including with government and parks personnel, where concerns were aired and information shared about threats to take over the provincial park next. Plans were made for undercover surveillance of the park and for an Emergency Response Team (ERT) to be stationed at the Pinery Provincial Park close to Grand Bend, some twelve kilometres away. It was also decided that Ron Fox, Special Adviser on First Nations in the Deputy Solicitor General's Office, should be included in updates on the occupation. Fox was a career OPP officer with the rank of inspector, who was considered to have had extensive experience with First Nations; some of the Six Nations of the Grand River Territory had been part of his patrol area. He was seconded to his government position in February of 1995 and directed to report operationally to the deputy solicitor general and deputy minister of Correctional Services and to the OPP only for administrative things like attendance, vacation credits, et cetera.

On August 28, Carson pulled together some senior officers to sketch out a tactical response to a possible occupation of Ipperwash Provincial Park: how many ERTs, the possible use of Tactics and Rescue Units (TRUs), the possibility of bringing in a light armoured vehicle and also some OPP watercraft to guard access to the park from the lake. On Friday, September 1, Carson convened a second, larger meeting of twenty officers. He began by saying that the goal was "to contain and negotiate a peaceful solution" to any occupation. He told the officers that no firearms had been used or threatened since the original occupation of the army base three years earlier. He drew on the results of an inventory they had done of available female officers. The plan was to deploy a lot of these women in the event of an occupation. He then detailed the units that would be involved: four ERTs, each with fifteen officers, at least one TRU team, a negotiations unit, an intelligence unit for gathering information and identifying the people involved in the occupation, plus a logistics team to coordinate all the vehicles and equipment involved. This team would have arranged for an ambulance to be on hand if that detail had been flagged, but it was not. Carson did contact St. John Ambulance about procuring the use of their communications vehicle, filled with telephone, radio signalling, and computer equipment. He did not mention an ambulance.

Carson then briefed some of Les Kobayashi's staff with the Ministry of Natural Resources (MNR), the department that ran Ipperwash Provincial Park. He reiterated that the OPP's goal was "to contain and negotiate." It was understood that the MNR would proceed with an injunction should any First Nations people occupy the park. By the end of that day, Carson had distributed fifteen copies of the Project Maple operations booklet. A Community Liaison Unit had been added, responsible for communicating with stakeholders, including local municipal officials and the chief of the Kettle and Stony Point band council. And an OPP incident command centre had been set up in the nearby town of Forest.

By 8:30 on the morning of September 5, Carson had already been in touch with Tom Bressette and learned that the chief and council did not support the occupation of the Ipperwash Provincial Park, which had taken place the previous evening. Nor did they question ownership of the park. Bressette told him about a burial ground there and the local knowledge of its having been disturbed by bulldozers during postwar work on the park. He also conveyed his impatience. As the tape in the command post recorded every word of his conversation with Carson, Bressette confided that he and the band council were "tired of these folks ... giving [us] a bad name," adding that "treating them with kid gloves isn't something ... they understand."

Carson gathered from this that there was "certainly not a very harmonious relationship [between] the occupiers and the Kettle Point band." Still, both he and his assistant commander, Mark Wright, felt that they had clarity from the official representatives of the First Nation involved.

At 9:00 a.m., the chief administrative officer for the local township of Bosanquet arrived at the command centre wanting to get an

update and to press for declaring a state of emergency in the muni-
cipality. Carson told him that the OPP had set up checkpoints to
monitor people entering the park area, and that preparations for an
injunction were being made. When he left, Carson asked Sergeant
Stan Korosec, head of the ERTs, to send officers door to door among
the neighbouring cottages assuring their owners of their, the OPP's,
presence.

The local member of the provincial legislature, Marcel Beaubien,
contacted Wade Lacroix, one of the OPP officers on the case and
someone to whom Beaubien had sold life insurance. Lacroix relayed
to Carson that Beaubien was "irate." He "wanted something done"
and was going to call the premier. Beaubien had taken action earlier
in the summer too. He had met with Lacroix and Carson on July 31,
after the barracks takeover, and followed up by sending a letter to Ontario Attorney General Harnick saying his constituents are "stressed
out and the situation is becoming unbearable ... Law enforcement is
basically non-existent and the OPP does not seem too keen to get
involved."

At 9:25 a.m., Carson convened a meeting of his senior officers, telling them that Chief Tom Bressette supported the OPP's position and
that the chief and band council were not asserting a land claim to
the park. He then focused his attention on arranging for more equipment, including helicopters for surveillance, night-vision goggles, and
a military-style light armoured vehicle – even if one had to be special
ordered directly from the GM factory in Detroit.

Shortly after noon, Brad Seltzer, in charge of the negotiations unit,
plus Mark Wright and Les Kobayashi, all wearing bulletproof vests,
approached the fence at the park asking to speak to their leader. The
idea was that Seltzer would begin some sort of dialogue of negotiation. Seltzer had no training in crisis negotiation, nor in First Nations
history or culture. The negotiation unit also lacked any communication plan outlining the kind of information to convey to the Indigenous people occupying the park, nor how this information might be
conveyed – whether by bullhorn, printed paper, or telephone.

No one would come to the fence to talk to them. So they went to
the army base and made contact with Bert Manning, who they'd
been told was acting as spokesperson. He said he would talk to the
elders about setting up some dialogue; they should come back the
next day. Meanwhile, he said, the people in the park were glad to get

their burial grounds back. Detective Sergeant Wright, in turn, informed Manning that the Aboriginal people were in the park unlawfully and that an injunction was being sought.

Early that afternoon, the mayor of the township issued a press release headlined "Reign of Terror Continues."

> "The current reign of terror in our community continues," Mayor Fred Thomas advised Council this afternoon, one day after a group of Indians [sic] illegally took over Ipperwash Provincial Park ...
>
> "First they kicked the Army out of the Army Camp and now they kicked the Province out of the Park. What's next?" Thomas wondered ... "The Federal Government assured me that all these terrorist activities would be confined within the perimeter of the Army Camp, but this hasn't happened." ...
>
> "I have heard rumours that people are buying guns to protect themselves and their families. Surely this is not a recipe for peace, order and good government," the Mayor stated.
>
> The Town is demanding ... action to remove the illegal occupiers from the land. "The laws of Canada and Ontario must be enforced equally for all Canadians."[3]

PREMIER MIKE HARRIS, "HAWKISH"

Midmorning that day in Toronto, Julie Jai convened a meeting of the Inter-Ministerial Committee on Aboriginal Emergencies (IMC) at the offices of the Ontario Native Affairs Secretariat (ONAS). She was the acting legal director of ONAS and chair of the IMC. She had called a meeting of the IMC in early August, having been contacted by the MNR about the possible occupation of Ipperwash Park. Participants had shared a lot of background information and discussed the possibility of negotiations, which the IMC had the authority to pursue. The meeting ended with a consensus to wait, watch, and see. Jai then went on holidays, returning on the morning of September 5.

The September 5 meeting brought together senior civil servants plus the political staff (executive assistants, or EAs) of the premier and relevant cabinet ministers. Protocol expected these people to confine themselves to observing and providing information from their ministers only. OPP Superintendent Ron Fox was also there, seconded to the Ministry of the Solicitor General. The meeting began with general information sharing. There had been no communication with the occupiers, so their demands were not yet known. Fox reported that there was no evidence of firearms and, according to meeting notes, added that "Carson says 'Use of alcohol quite high.'" There were precedents of legitimate ceremonial activity by First Nations people in provincial parks, including Ipperwash. The existence of burial grounds was mentioned but met with a comment that even if true, this didn't have a bearing on title to the land. The prior questioning of that title's legitimacy was raised, but it was agreed that title remained with the province, and that seemed to settle that.

There was then some discussion about an injunction, the then-still-ongoing standoff at Gustafsen Lake in BC, and the danger of the situation at Ipperwash escalating, especially if precipitous action was taken. But since the park was officially empty and closed for the season, people agreed there seemed to be no urgency to act.

Deb Hutton, the EA for the newly elected premier, Mike Harris, spoke up, saying: "[The] Premier is hawkish on this issue," and feels "'we're being tested.'" She felt that action was needed immediately.

Jeff Bangs, EA to the minister of Natural Resources, reminded the meeting of the Statement of Political Relationship that had been developed under the previous NDP government of Premier Bob Rae. It was a framework for any future provincial government dealings with First Nations Peoples. Negotiated between the government and First Nations leaders from across the province, it moved beyond Indian Act bands and band councils by recognizing the inherent First Nations right of self-government. It also committed the province together with local First Nations to implement that right by "respecting treaty relationships" and the processes associated with them.

Julie Jai: "Probably the most significant thing about this document is that it says that Ontario recognizes that under the Constitution of Canada, First Nations have an inherent right to self-government, within the Canadian Constitutional framework ... And it was a kind of symbol that, I remember hearing reference to kind of government-to-government dealings ... And then the long document that's attached to it ... is a guide that was prepared by the Native Affairs Secretariat for the public as well as internally for staff and all the ministries of the government to set out what is this, why did we do this, what are treaty rights, what are Aboriginal rights ... So it's a whole primer from beginning to end; it's almost fifty pages.

"But [with the change of government] I think that there was a general assumption that they would probably not be endorsing the Statement of Political Relationship, given the position that their party had taken ... during the election and then, I think they were quite consistent with it once they formed the government, indicating that Aboriginal people don't have special rights.

"So that's sort of diametrically opposed to what's in the Statement of Political Relationship."[4]

The statement was not legally binding. Still, no policy had been developed to replace it. As Bangs later told the Ipperwash Inquiry: "It was still in existence, still on the books ... Still an existing live document, and I thought we needed to be mindful of it and perhaps follow some of the elements of it ...

"I don't recall that it was [taken up as a discussion point]. We began talking about other things. My comment was noted, and we moved on."

Another political staffer then drew an analogy to having a bunch of Hells Angels set up camp on a person's front lawn and asked the meeting: "Would you not be able to call the police and have them removed?"

Ron Fox mentioned the long-standing common law concept of the colour of right, the civil right defence against a possible charge of using or possessing a property. As he told the Inquiry: "I recall indicating to the committee that what needed to be examined is what the rationale was of the people that were there, if they felt they had some reasonable entitlement to be there. I did speak about colour of right at that meeting ... I think generally the view of the meeting, on the part of MNR and Ms. Hutton, was that ... it was purely a trespass to property and should be dealt with in that fashion, or a criminal mischief with respect to interfering with the lawful use or enjoyment of property."

Deb Hutton told the Inquiry: "The ownership of the park, as I understood it, and the clear title of the park meant that Colour of Right was not ... applicable in this situation as it related to the occupation."

Ministry of the Attorney General lawyer Elizabeth Christie then outlined the legal options available to the government. She mentioned mischief charges under the Criminal Code and trespass charges under the Trespass to Property Act and Provincial Park and Public Lands Acts. She also explained the difference between applying for an ordinary injunction, which would take two weeks and require serving notice, versus an emergency "ex parte" injunction, which could be granted immediately and served without prior notice. A discussion of the feasibility and urgency of the latter option was followed by discussion of a communications plan that would be taken back for senior bureaucrat and politicians' approval. Some disagreement over including reference to the possible existence of burial grounds at Ipperwash, which Ron Fox supported, was resolved in favour of omitting this. Meeting notes referred to Deb Hutton having intervened forcefully on this point, saying: "Strategic imperative – this government treats non-Aboriginal and Aboriginal people the same."

Ten years later, Elizabeth Christie told the Ipperwash Inquiry that she had been personally disturbed at these comments because they "demonstrated an unnerving ignorance of constitutional law and ... my understanding was that, based on the Constitution and the Charter and jurisprudence, that we don't necessarily treat Aboriginal and non-Aboriginal people the same ... in certain circumstances."

Deb Hutton told the Inquiry: "Because the ownership issue was clear, as I understood it, and would continue to be clear even in the existence of a burial ground, and given the chief's lack of support, reinforced that for me as well; that in this very specific issue we were dealing with an issue that was not Aboriginal – it was not a land claim issue ... I believed the occupation was illegal."

The views of Deb Hutton, the spokesperson for the premier, prevailed. As Dave Moran, EA to the attorney general, told the Ipperwash Inquiry: "The impression that we were given was that this was strictly a law enforcement issue and that other than the fact that the people who had taken over the park were Natives, that's just basically where the Native issues ended ... It was strictly a law enforcement issue. The focus of the discussion was all on law enforcement ... or ownership ... matters."

When the Inter-Ministerial Committee meeting ended, the minister of Natural Resources, Chris Hodgson, was designated the interim government spokesman. His office was tasked with informing the public that the province had clear title to the park, that the occupiers were trespassing, and that steps would be taken to remove them as soon as possible. The meeting notes recorded that the OPP would have "the discretion as to how to proceed" with this. A next meeting was scheduled for 9:00 a.m. the next day. At this point at least, the IMC was not choosing to exercise its authority to set up a negotiating process.

ACTING LIKE "ANIMALS" AND "JERKS"

By early afternoon, Carson had arranged for an OPP boat from Grand Bend to be stationed offshore in Lake Huron to monitor the beach and a second, larger vessel from Kincardine to be deployed at night. The bugs in relaying images from the video surveillance cameras in the provincial park buildings to the OPP intelligence unit in Grand Bend were still being worked out. And Carson was still making phone calls to secure a light armoured vehicle plus Nomex flame resistant suits in the event the occupiers used another "incendiary device." (During a short confrontation between the OPP and the occupiers on the night of September 4, sixteen-year-old Nicholas Cottrelle had reportedly tossed a lit, flare-like piece of firework at the police; mischief charges against him were pending.)

Meanwhile, Carson's second-in-command, Mark Wright, was back and forth on the phone with Orillia General Headquarters trying to line up surveillance helicopters ASAP. He told the officer in charge: "There's real potential for one of our guys to get hit ... And we're really uncomfortable sending our guys in there without somebody overhead." When asked if they needed extra weaponry, Wright turned to ERT unit leader Stan Korosec and asked: "What about when we start bringing the Road Warriors down here? We going to have enough guns and everything for them? Do we need more guns?"

At 1:00 p.m., MPP Beaubien faxed a draft press release to Bill King, the person in the premier's office responsible for liaising with MPPs. Beaubien proposed sending it out at 3:00 p.m. The draft release began with extensive quotes from a letter to the editor in the local *Forest Standard* newspaper written by Kettle and Stony Point band councillor Gerald ("Booper") George, published on August 30, just before the Labour Day weekend. In it, George criticized what he called the "army camp Indians," acting "like animals" and "jerks," saying that the situation at Camp Ipperwash "reminded me of the L.A. Riots."[5]

Beaubien's draft went on to say: "We are not dealing with your decent native citizen. We are dealing with thugs ... Enough is enough ... How can we negotiate with irresponsible, law-breaking dissidents[?] We must come to our senses and take back control." King advised Beaubien against sending out the release; Beaubien listened, and did not.

At his 4:45 p.m. briefing at the command centre, Carson passed on what Inspector Ron Fox had relayed to him from the IMC meeting in Toronto,[6] including that the people occupying the park were to receive "no different treatment from anybody else." At his 6:00 p.m. briefing, he told his team that they were getting "heat from the political side."

PICNIC TABLE INCIDENT

At around 10:00 p.m., officers were alerted to some activity outside the fence at Ipperwash Park. Picnic tables from the park had been stacked up in the sandy parking lot at the "road allowance" end of Army Camp Road, which led to and provided direct car access to the beach. They radioed in for reinforcements. When they arrived, some kind of altercation occurred with the protestors who, all by then inside the fence, began throwing stones at the officers, hitting one of the cruiser's windows. By 11:00 p.m., the officers had withdrawn.

One of them, Constable Jacklin, contacted ERT unit leader Korosec to fill him in on what happened, telling him about the OPP being "pelted" with rocks.

Korosec responded: "Yeah. They were baited."

Jacklin: "Yup."

Korosec: "Well, live and learn, live and learn. This – their day will fucking come."

Jacklin: "Yeah."

Korosec: "I was talking to Mark Wright tonight."

Jacklin: "Hmmmm."

Korosec: "We want to amass a fucking army."

Jacklin: "Hmmm."

Korosec: "A real fucking army and do this – do these fuckers big time. But I don't want to talk about it because I'll get all hyped up."

Jacklin: "And you won't be able to sleep."

Korosec: "And I won't be able to sleep. Okay. What time is it? Quarter to twelve. Okay."

Jacklin: "Back to bed."

Korosec: "Steady up."

Jacklin: "Okay."[7]

"THIS CHANGES THINGS"

At 8:00 a.m. on September 6, Kent Skinner, TRU team leader, received information, called in at 11:00 p.m. on September 5, of "bursts of gunfire" heard in the park or vicinity; possibly fifty to one hundred rounds, possibly automatic weaponry. He shared this as-yet unverified information with the TRU team, including Acting Sergeant Ken ("Tex") Deanne, his second-in-command, adding: "This changes things."

At 8:40 a.m., two ERTs (thirty officers) arrived at Ipperwash Park to pick up the picnic tables. These were still in a semicircle outside the park fence. Dudley George and fourteen-year-old J.T. Cousins were sitting on one, drinking coffee. A helicopter hovered overhead providing additional cover for the police. Ten officers pointed their Ruger Mini-14 assault rifles at Dudley and J.T. while the others moved forward, holding up Plexiglas shields as they advanced. They loaded the tables into a MNR truck without incident and left. They also filed a warrant for Dudley George's arrest for possessing stolen property (the picnic tables) and mischief. His name was entered into the national police information system.

Inspector John Carson spent time discussing the possibility of additional equipment, such as a pepper-spray "fogger," ATVs for beach patrols, canine units, and a new expandable twenty-six-inch steel baton (known as ASP batons, the acronym for Armament Systems and Procedures, Inc., which manufactures them). Carson asked that these be distributed to all ERT officers to carry on their belts.

Carson also spent time on the phone with Tim McCabe, the MNR lawyer who was looking for grounds to justify an emergency ex parte injunction. Carson talked about the rock throwing during the previous night's picnic table incident but held back on the reports of automatic or semiautomatic gunfire. His intelligence officer, Don Bell, had said that the reliability of this information was "still up in the air." What to him was a reliable source had also said that there was no evidence of weapons on site. At the end of the call, Carson promised to fax over the list of the twenty-six people in the park who had been identified so far, partly through helicopter surveillance.

DND Captain Doug Smith showed up to offer his services. He had acted as the army's liaison with us Stoney Pointers at the army camp after July 29 and had earlier arranged for Oneida Nation conflict-resolution mediators, Bob Antone and Bruce Elijah, to provide some cultural awareness and sensitivity training for army staff at Ipperwash. Carson said he might pursue Smith's offer in a couple of days.

Another Indigenous mediator, Cyndy Elder from Manitoulin Island, called and left a message, also offering her services and mentioning her recent experience at Gustafsen Lake. Carson was too busy to return her call.

In Toronto, Julie Jai began a 9:30 a.m. meeting of the Inter-Ministerial Committee with updates. Ron Fox mentioned the picnic table incident but nothing about reports of gunfire. Peter Sturdy, reporting for the MNR, passed on what Les Kobayashi had heard at the OPP command centre about "automatic gunfire." This would have been the "bursts of gunfire" report from the previous night, which had not been confirmed. Sturdy also said his staff were being peppered with calls from local residents, expressing concern, fear, anger, and anxiety. He was also alarmed that the OPP was urging MNR staff to wear bulletproof vests.

Julie Jai asked Dave Carson, a staffer with the ONAS, whom she had asked to check into the burial grounds, to report. According to meeting notes, he mentioned "unverified" burial grounds at Ipperwash Park, then reviewed official procedures under the Heritage Act and the Cemeteries Act in the event of an "unapproved" cemetery being found. A complete file on the human remains that had been disturbed in 1950 at the Ipperwash Provincial Park, and the verification of these as Indigenous, was in a filing cabinet in the basement of the Whitney Block almost next door. Its existence was rediscovered later.

The meeting notes indicate no discussion of the burial grounds question.

Tim McCabe, reporting for the attorney general, provided an update on the injunction question, saying they did not have sufficient grounds for an ex parte injunction, so a civil injunction would be pursued, with an application going forward as early as Friday. According to meeting notes, Deb Hutton objected, saying: "The Premier's view is that the longer the occupiers are there the greater the opportunity they have to garner support ... he wants them out in a day or two." Deb Hutton had briefed Premier Harris on the previous day's meeting late that evening. Harris had spent the day attending the Canadian Open (golf tournament).

The discussion then shifted away from an injunction and toward Criminal Code options. Fox cautioned against this, repeating what he had said earlier about colour of right. There was debate about whether the issue was a strictly law-and-order matter for the police or a government matter. Deb Hutton suggested that the matter should go to cabinet. She added: "I suspect Premier Harris is willing to take the lead."

The matter was not taken up in cabinet, but at an informal meeting Mike Harris convened immediately afterward, in the private dining room next door. Only the attorney general, solicitor general, and minister of Natural Resources, plus some selected staff, attended; no official notes were taken. As the attorney general, Charles Harnick, arrived for the meeting and entered the room, he overheard the premier declaring loudly: "I want the fucking Indians out of the park!" (He acknowledged that this was what he had heard only when under oath at the Ipperwash Inquiry. Whenever he had been questioned about this statement earlier in the legislature, he had always responded: "I have no knowledge of ...")

Harris also asked about the OPP's failure to secure the park on September 4. Ron Fox took this as criticism of the OPP and shared this with Carson on the phone after the meeting.

The call to Carson was mainly about the injunction and the government's decision to go the ex parte emergency route. A lawyer in the Crown Law Office had been instructed to make the application that day, if possible. They needed evidence of "emergent circumstances" to support it.

Carson reviewed some of the events that might help make the case, mentioning "an altercation through the night with the cruiser windows being smashed ... Picnic tables on the sandy parking lot ... [still unverified] gunfire that was heard back in the military base through the night ... Cars being driven in [an] erratic manner inside the park ... When you put all those factors together, there's such a progression of events that, hopefully, you would have enough [justification] ... for an emergent order."

"A Report of Semiautomatic Weapon Fire in the Park"

At 6:40 p.m., MPP Marcel Beaubien walked into the command post to see Carson insisting that "something has to be done to handle the situation." Word also came in that local property owners were organizing some action themselves and were gathering at an MNR parking lot down the road from Ipperwash Park where the OPP's Tactical Operations Centre was set up. Carson sent his assistant incident commander, Mark Wright, to check it out. Wright found the mayor, Fred Thomas, and a crowd of thirty to forty men and women, local cottage and property owners, many with signs, getting ready to march to Ipperwash Park to take on the occupiers themselves. Wright managed to talk them down.

When he left, at around 7:30 p.m., Wright drove past the intersection of East Parkway Drive and Army Camp Road, at the entrance to the Ipperwash Provincial Park. He stopped when he noticed some eight to ten Aboriginal men in the sandy parking lot from which the picnic tables had been removed that morning. Half of them had what looked like baseball bats or axe handles in their hands. When he asked what the men were doing, he was told to leave. Wright, who was dressed in civilian clothes, decided to do this because he recognized Stewart ("Worm") George, who was walking toward him, and worried that George would, in turn, recognize him. He drove up Army Camp Road and stopped at the police checkpoint halfway along it, Checkpoint C, telling the OPP officers there that he thought "things are escalating" and telling them to "be careful." Wright said much the same thing when he stopped at the next checkpoint, at the intersection of Army Camp Road and Highway 21. While he was there, someone at Checkpoint C radioed in "that a civilian's car had been damaged by a rock thrown by 'Natives on the road.'" Wright then drove on, heading to Forest. En route, he radioed in an update from his parking lot encounter: "They've got some bats and stuff in their hand[s] and apparently they damaged some – an individual's vehicle. So we got some mischief right now. And wilful damage." He radioed in a second time to tell Sergeant Korosec, ERT unit commander, to hold back the day shift as the night shift arrived to replace them. Just in case.

At the command centre in Forest, he briefed Acting Incident Commander Dale Linton. John Carson had gone off duty at 7:00 p.m. and was having supper at a private home in town. Linton talked about bringing in the "B team with helmets and K-9" (canine unit). Wright consulted with Carson on the phone. Carson did not want action taken until the vehicle damage report could be verified. Detective Constable Chris Martin, who was monitoring the Ipperwash Park video cameras from the Grand Bend OPP headquarters, relayed seeing a Native male inside the park gatehouse kiosk with the blinds down and the door closed. Periodically, he would peer out the window. Martin could not tell if the man was armed. Detective Sergeant Richardson, reviewing this information with Sergeant Korosec, considered the behaviour suspicious.

When Detective Constable Mark Dew arrived for his shift at the Forest Command Centre at 7:55 p.m., Sergeant Richardson sent him out to help check out the vehicle damage incident Constable Poole at Checkpoint C had reported. On the way there, he stopped at Checkpoint D, where the ERT officers told him: "Women and children were leaving ... because there was going to be trouble" that night.

At Checkpoint C, he met with the man whose vehicle had been damaged. His name was Gerald ("Booper") George, the member of the Kettle and Stony Point band council who had published that damning letter in the local paper at the end of August. George repeated what he had already told Poole: that the occupiers had guns and were making Molotov cocktails.

Dew contacted the command centre immediately after this interview to say that someone had reported hunting rifles and semiautomatic guns, and that they might be building gas bombs. He omitted naming George – "I was concerned for his safety." He was also unaware of the letter George had written in the local paper just over a week earlier.

At 8:41 p.m., he followed up with a more detailed report, beginning: "I just talked to a fella down here who's been in and eyeballed some of the weaponry that they have ... He has seen four SKS ... Yeah, those are Russian semiautomatics ... They have thirty round detachable clips and a couple of them have fixed ten round clips ... They've got two Ruger Mini-14s with thirty round mags."

"How big are the clips?"

"Three-zero."

"Okay. Thank you, buddy ... I'll let Stan [Korosec] know and he can let them know what's going on."

Sergeant Rob Graham, who had taken the call from Dew, passed on the information to Inspector Linton. There was no analysis of this information and its reliability; nor had there been over the reports of "bursts of gunfire" heard somewhere at the back of the army base the previous night. As the Ipperwash Inquiry made clear, unverified raw data was fed directly to the incident commander.

At around this time (at 8:25 p.m.), Wright took a call from Tim McCabe, the government lawyer trying to establish grounds for bringing an application for an ex parte injunction before a judge the next morning. "The shit's coming down now," he told McCabe. "We got major trouble right now." When McCabe asked what he meant, Wright said: "Well, they're moving ... they're coming out for a fight down to the road, so we're [taking] all the marines down now."[8]

He then reviewed the possible evidence to justify an injunction, telling McCabe the OPP "had a report of automatic weapon fire in the park ... and they've got about eight guys on the edge of the road with bats in their hand ... And that's a public county road access, so that's mischief ... And [regarding the Gerald George incident] they've trashed a car that went by, so we've got wilful damage. We've got possession of dangerous weapon. And we got four ERT teams and a TRU team and two canine units going down there to do battle right now."

Mark Wright also filled Carson in on the phone. He said that Aboriginal people had "pelted" a car. He told him that the ERT day shift and canine team were present. He asked Carson what he should say to Linton if he asks.

Carson replied: "Well, it's not my ..." (The rest was inaudible on the tape.)

Wright: "Don't you say we go get those fucking guys?"

He mentioned that Linton was considering calling in the TRU. Carson immediately replied: "You advise him I should be notified." A TRU is considered a last resort, Justice Linden explained in his Inquiry report. Its officers have the training to use sophisticated paramilitary weaponry, propelling bullets with greater accuracy and more deadly force.

Carson told the Inquiry: "The criteria for calling out a tactical team normally involves a threat to life ... People on the roadway with a baseball bat falls far short of that criteria."

There was discussion at the command post about preparing the ERTs to come together as one larger Crowd Management Unit (CMU). They needed a trained incident commander to lead the CMU; Linton asked ERT unit head, Stan Korosec, to call in Wade Lacroix. At Linton's request, Korosec also contacted Acting Staff Sergeant Kent Skinner, TRU team leader, to bring the TRU team up for a briefing. He told Skinner that some First Nations people at Army Camp Road and East Parkway Drive had "trashed" a car with "baseball bats" as it passed the intersection. Skinner shared this intel with his officers, believing it to be accurate.

When Lacroix arrived at the command post, he was told much the same thing: "A civilian car pelted with stones and hit by baseball bats as it attempted to pass the park." In his mind, this was the trigger for deploying the CMU.

Linton called Carson, telling him: "We're heating up big time. I just thought I would let you know." He mentioned "about eight guys on the road," and a damaged car, saying they were just waiting for a statement from the victim. "So we just got a statement now. She says that they were hassling her." (None of this was ever substantiated. The only corroborated incident was a single rock thrown at a single person's car: Gerald George's.) Linton continued: "Now they've got the school bus down in that corner ... They're in the kiosk with the windows down so they're waiting for us to do something. So I just – they called the TRU team in and ... well, I'll wait till I get the statement. We're probably going to go down and arrest that group of eight or so people blocking the roadway, and there's no doubt ... they're waiting for something. So it's a little vulnerable. So I'll suit the TRU up heavy and put them in. So they're en route here now."

Carson told Linton not to use the TRU or even call them in. Then: "Are you asking my advice or are you just informing me here? We better get this straight." Linton replied, "No, we need to discuss this."

"Okay. Do you want me to come in?"

"Well ... why shouldn't we use, like what we've got ... and you've got people in the kiosk pulling the blinds all down and I think there's ... a threat here of maybe sniper fire, or like they're doing something inside getting ready for us."

Carson said: "Okay. Well, okay. Well, that's fine. Let's evacuate those houses [nearby] if you think ... there's a threat of that nature. But don't go in there with TRU. If you go in with TRU and somebody gets hurt, we have nobody else to get them out."

Linton reassured him that he was only asking the TRU officers to come in.

Carson said he would not even do that. "If you bring that team up, you got to be ready to deploy them."

After the call, Carson headed back to the command post. At about the same time, Linton asked Korosec to contact the TRU team with instructions to turn around. By the time he got through, Skinner and his second-in-command, Ken ("Tex") Deanne, were nearly at Forest. Korosec also reported that, "We got a big gathering down at the end of Army Camp Road. They trashed a private vehicle that went by, with bats ... They're armed with baseball bats and whatnot at this intersection."

At 9:09 p.m., TRU commander Skinner relayed the as-yet still un-verified weapons information he had received from Inspector Dale Linton, originally from Gerald George, to Deanne and the other TRU officers: four imitation AK-47s ("knock-offs" but considered "just as dangerous," "just as lethal"), Ruger Mini-14s, scoped hunting rifles, and Molotov cocktails. In Skinner's view, the probable existence of these weapons, combined with earlier reports of automatic weapons fire and damage to a civilian's car, raised the likelihood of his unit being deployed that night.

By then, the CMU officers were kitted up in shin, thigh, and fore-arm guards, plus ASP batons, shields, and helmets with visors and audio gear through which they could be connected to command control communications on the OPP's total access channel. Skinner, Deanne, and the other TRU officers had assault rifles and semiautomatic pistols. They also wore bulletproof vests.

Carson was clear in his briefing: The TRU were to flank the CMU officers, providing cover only. The CMU's purpose was to move the Indigenous people back into Ipperwash Park. CMU officers were to only arrest "any demonstrators" who refused to leave the sandy parking lot at the edge of the intersection of Army Camp Road and East Parkway Drive. They would be charged with unlawful assembly and mischief. "Under no circumstances" he said, were CMU officers to "go into the park."

There were no instructions about letting us – the "fucking Indians" and the "fuckers" in the eyes of at least some of those giving the orders – know that we would only be asked to return to the park. No one thought to tell us that we would be safe – left alone – as long as we were inside the park. We remained ignorant of this important fact.

At 9:46 p.m., Inspector Linton called OPP Superintendent Tony Parkin to update him, reporting that the OPP "had a whole list of automatic weapons that somebody gave us this evening ... that's supposed to be down there" and going on to mention the possibility of sniper fire. Superintendent Parkin asked what the officers at Grand Bend could see on the surveillance video. Linton said the images were blurry and the movements of the occupiers could not be seen. The First Nations people, he said "are outside the fence ... lighting fires" and they have "clubs and stuff ... So it looks like tonight's the night. They're revved up for action. Their women and kids are leaving. It really surprised [me] that they'd be this aggressive."

Parkin remarked: "They're probably all boozed up, they've probably been drinking."

He asked if the OPP plan was to remain outside the park. Linton assured him it was.

Parkin also shared his surprise that an unverified report of possible automatic weapons having been fired the previous night had gone "up through the MNR side" not just to the minister of Natural Resources but also to the Deputy Solicitor General's Office. Parkin had subsequently spoken directly to the solicitor general, however, "and they were more than pleased with what the OPP was doing, so there's no problem there."

"Just make sure that you and John control it," Parkin told Linton as he wrapped things up.

Get in touch, he said, "if things start to really take a tumble."

At 10:27 p.m., the CMU marched down Eastern Parkway Drive toward Ipperwash Provincial Park, the TRU flanking them on either side. There were thirty-two officers in the unit. They were followed by an eight-officer arrest team, plus two canine units. Two prisoner vans followed behind.

CHAPTER NINE

September 5–6, 1995, from Our Point of View

For Kevin Simon, the events that led to our brother, our nephew, our cousin Dudley being shot to death with nothing or nobody seeming able to prevent it had started much, much earlier. If things started "to take a tumble" like the OPP superintendent said, it had begun at least twenty-four hours earlier. It started during the confrontation with the OPP over the stacked-up picnic tables the previous evening. Kevin, Dudley, and some of the other guys had set these up in the sandy parking area outside the fence on September 5 to block access through it to the beach where Army Camp Road ended at East Parkway Drive.

Kevin: "We had been through a lot of problems with people coming in behind us along the beach."

Marlin: "Red necks or whatever. They'd pull up in that area and start yelling obscenities or whatever, wanting to start trouble. So we'd just close it off."

Kevin: "When we went into the park, we had talked about closing that off completely so that people couldn't continue doing that, and we didn't really feel that it was that big of a deal because it was part of our land too, we felt. And it was, it was just access to the park, basically," beyond where the paved road ends.

"We had quite a few tables out there – to keep people from going [down] onto the beach."

Leland (age thirteen): "[We put them] so they'd be like the long way, right across there ... making a blockade, with picnic tables. And they were, like piling them up ... And then a cruiser came."

Marlin: "The police wanted us to go back into the park and told us to leave – leave the parking lot area or whatever, and we said, 'Why?' You know, 'We're not doing anything. It's a public roadway. We're just sitting here.'"

"And he was still standing there and another cruiser kind of come up."

Kevin: "And he inched his way right up to where the picnic tables were and as soon as he basically got close enough to hit one, you could see him give a shot of gas and push that table. And there's people sitting on that table ... and you could see the table, it skidded a good couple of feet."

Marlin: "And everybody went and helped ... and people started pushing back with the picnic table, and pushing back toward the police car, and ended up throwing the picnic table right on top of the police car. Right on the hood."

Kevin: "And that's basically when he backed up and left ... The other cruisers too."

Leland: "[We] piled the picnic tables back up."

Kevin: "In a semicircle ... We had the tables and then [inside the fence] the fire and then the lake ... half a dozen [of us], but there was probably more because there was quite a few kids running around ... Wes had some of those ... little firecrackers. Just small things that make a boom ... Weren't nothing fancy about them but he was throwing those too."

Then the police came back; a bunch of them.

Kevin: "They come up there with, I guess they were like riot squad or whatever – guys with shields and clubs. They come into the parking lot, beat their clubs a bit, spread out."

One of officers hit the fence with his baton, saying: "We want to try these out."

They were metal; you could tell by the sound they made hitting the fence.

Kevin: "There was one person that was doing a lot of the talking ... saying stuff like 'Welcome to Canada' and all this sort of stuff ... There were others saying stuff too ... All sorts of stuff. 'Wahoos,' 'Wagon burners' – any kind of stuff like that – just degrading references to our ancestry ... They weren't shy about it and didn't try to cover it up by any means.

They were outright stating that ... and then they pointed out Dudley, that was what really stuck out ... knowing that, before when we were living on the ranges, he was subject to a lot of harassment from the police driving by with their spotlights and sirens and whatnot."

Marlin: "There was one big police officer that was walking around, and he was playing with his big baton, or ASP baton or whatever ... and he was asking which one of us guys wanted to be the first. Who was going to be the first one out, get dragged out? 'We're going to take care of you guys. Who's going to be first?' And then he looks at Dudley, and [says,] 'Dudley, you're going to be the first one.'

"And it was like, 'whoa.' And we were right face-to-face with the police, and I was standing right beside Dudley, kind of right behind him. And I kind of went down behind him and grabbed some sand and threw it right in that police officer's face. And right away, the police officer behind him pulls out this big can of mace and starts spraying.

"Everybody on our side of the fence kind of split, and we just started picking up rocks and throwing them at the police ... and that's when they started to leave."

Kevin: "I had an uneasy feeling ... after hearing Dudley being threatened. I made the decision that night I'd be staying there to witness if they come back to come good on what they had threatened. I never went to work that day."

Stewart: "It was in the morning, and Robert Isaac ... come and told me that they needed some bodies down at the park ... because they took the picnic tables away ... Somebody had an AM radio plugged in over at the store, and they were listening to the news, and they were saying ... they were trying to get a court injunction. I don't know who was trying to get it."

Kevin: "And the police were saying something about an injunction ... Whoever was telling me about it, they didn't understand what it was either."

Stewart: "I figured I'd probably end up in jail ... for a little while. For trespassing; something like that."

"Bring the Kids Back, and We'll Have a Picnic"

Marlin: "Nothing really changed. The kids were just playing around ... trying to be useful, and women were making lunches and stuff like that."

Stewart: "The kids, they had a mirror they got, I think it was out of one of the bathrooms, and they had it sitting out on a picnic table reflecting the sun toward the police when they were out on the road ... Just for fun; they were just young kids."

Leland: "Yeah, to be annoying."

Marlin: "Uncle Abe, he wanted certain jobs done ... After [last] night when everything happened, everybody was kind of, kind of getting worried ... They'd been trying, it seemed like trying to pick a fight or something ... Everybody figured that the police were going to try something again this night.

"My job was to fuel things up. So I loaded up all the gas cans I could find and started moving those all over, stashing them all over the army base ... in case ... if the police moved in and we got pushed off, we'd have some gas around, for the vehicles, patrolling around and stuff. And I got the bus running again and parked that down there. The maintenance shed was right there, and fuel pumps. I was pumping gas out of there into the bus. And there was a helicopter flying around. It would fly over and whenever it seen people, it would just come in, just hover over. And a doorway [of the helicopter] was open, and there was a guy with a big camera ... and he was aiming it all over, whoever was around, pointing it right at people that were sitting around. And this helicopter was coming right down, it was making big dust storms. Wind was blowing everything all over. Anything that wasn't nailed down pretty much was blowing all over."

J.R.: "It kept coming after me, kind of to get a picture of me because I was trying to hide behind a tree."

Bonnie: "It was in the morning, probably about 10–10:30, that I first went down there ... It was a really nice day out. There was a nice breeze coming off the lake, and the sun was shining ...

"I was uneasy with the policemen behind with all the guns, and the helicopter, and they had a gun there ... and Dudley says: 'Don't be afraid ... They're not going to do anything with us in here ... They don't shoot anybody that don't have no weapons.'"

Kevin: "She was basically worried; you could tell. She was talking about the police ... being built up further and saying that the roads are being blocked ... At one point she was, basically along the lines of telling us that we should be leaving or preparing for the worst ... I'm not too sure her exact words, but she knew it wasn't, wasn't going to be good."

Bonnie: "And Dudley was kind of laughing because he said they were really mad at him because he teases them. He was that kind of person, pretty silly. He would do things. He said, they got mad when he mooned them ... It didn't happen when I was there; he was just telling me ... He yelled at them, and they'd yell back ... He told me, the guys who were there, he says they told me that when they get in here, he's going to be the first to get it ...

"I went to my car, and I got a couple of eagle feathers I've always had in my car that was given to me by an elder from way up north, and that person told me to carry them. And I gave them to Glenn, 'I want you to have these, you and the boys down here.' And when the helicopter seen me going to the car, it came real low again ... They were right over us, so low that the dust was all around, and they were taking pictures but it was two eagle feathers on a piece of hide ... and Glenn held them up in the air to them so they could see what it was ...

"And I asked Dudley and Glenn and them, 'what do you need?' And they said, 'we need some food and cigarettes.' So I said, 'okay, I'll go and get some' ... And they said, 'why don't you bring the kids back and we'll have a picnic,' he says."

Janet (Cloud): "It was also a time to get our kids ready for school. So we were preparing that day making sure the kids had clothes and their backpacks and all the things you do when you send them to school."

Kevin: "I went back and forth [up to the barracks, down to the park area through the day] ... just travelling around." Marcia, Kevin's mother, wanted to bring a camper trailer down to the park, but she ran out of time.

Marcia: "It was a very uneasy day because we saw the massive buildup of police – way beyond anything I've ever seen. And there were rumours that they were going to come and put us out of there ... And we thought they could come and attack us in the barracks ...

"It was hard because we didn't have telephones. We didn't have the ability to communicate with the outside world.

"I would go in and out of there [the park] and – as long as I could see my sons and see that they were okay, I would come back away."

J.R.: "I ended up spending most of the day just hanging around with Dudley ... riding around with Dudley. It was just an old worn-out car that wasn't even roadworthy. He was riding around in that with Robert Isaac driving. They were doin' donuts in front of the TV cameras.

"People were bringing in donations – sandwiches and juice, and I was going back and forth, taking stuff down – paper plates and napkins ... Someone had a radio on and there was something about a state of emergency was declared. The feeling I got; I don't know if you can describe it: a buildup of pressure inside. There were cops everywhere. You could see them all day long. They were watching us. They were very close to us, with their sidearms on.

"I felt: 'trouble's comin'.' Everyone got closer together, not to be far apart."

Several people helped move a dumpster in front of the main gate to keep the OPP from forcing their way in. Others collected rocks, sticks, and baseball bats out of people's cars.

Marlin: "People always ride around with bats and stuff in their cars just in case something ever happened. Because there was, like, not just *a* redneck person, there was usually a group of them that come down ... from around here."

Bonnie came back midafternoon with her husband, Fred, two of her daughters, Gail and Barb, plus eight grandchildren. They rode in Fred's big family van. "So we got our food and we got our pop and everything, and we went all the way back in, and they stopped us again, at the same stop [Checkpoint C, partway down Army Camp Road] and we went back and set up [on] a table ...

"And the helicopter, they followed us back in again, and the helicopter was right over when the kids were getting out. And they were taking pictures again ... And it would come back periodically again, real low, and the dust would all come up ... but we still ate our supper.

"The last time I seen Dudley, he was sitting on the corner of the picnic table talking to us, my husband and I ... He was proud of himself having a sit-in down here to let people know that this was a burial ground for our ancestors."

Gina: "We were just sitting around having a barbecue. Life was good; really good – until [her older brother] Bernard came running up: 'You guys are surrounded. The shit's hittin' the fan. They're shuttin' down the highway. They're evacuating the cottages.' As soon as he said that, most of the women and children went up to the barracks. And then it just got worse."

J.T.: "I got told that all the women and children were supposed to leave the park and go back to the barracks. There were quite a few people that were saying that." But he stayed.

"I wanted to support my people."

Marlin: "He [Bernard] come walking up, and he says something to the effect like, I can't turn my back on you guys. You know, you guys are my brothers, and I come down here to help out.

"I'm like, holy why? And he, well, he wouldn't say ... He kind of said that he was talking with the chief and councillors and he knew something was going to happen."

BADGERS IN THE PARK

Tom Bressette: "Mr. Carson called me quite regularly, and they come down to the community, and they were always asking questions, like 'What's going on inside there?' 'Do they have any weapons? Do they have this or that?' And I always told them directly what I heard. People tell me they've seen them ...

"Mr. Beaubien [the MPP] is another one who was always calling me and asking me what was going on ... At one point he asked me to go to his office, and I went to his office, and I had a discussion with him, and he had pretty much made up his mind already what he wanted to do."

He'd had a call from Assembly of First Nations national chief Ovide Mercredi in August, offering to help mediate: "I told him I can negotiate with the government myself. What are you gonna do for me that I can't do?"

Around lunchtime on September 6, he got a call from his friend Bob Watts. Watts had been the executive director of the Union of Ontario Indians before forming his own consulting firm. He had done some consulting work for Tom and the Kettle and Stony Point band and had also worked for the ONAS and had sometimes attended Inter-Ministerial Committee meetings (chaired by Julie Jai). Watts had been tipped off by someone in the Native Affairs Secretariat.

"Mr. Watts told me that he had heard from an individual who was in a meeting with the premier and several other people, ministers, and basically what he heard him say was, Mr. Harris basically stated to someone, 'Get those f'ing Indians out of the park even if we got to draw guns to do it ...'

"After I got the call from Bob Watts, I called the local radio station [in Sarnia]. The lady's always on there saying if you have any news, call in. Lee Michaels is her name. I called her and told her what I had heard, and she said, 'well, what would you like to say to people?' And I said, 'I would suggest that people start to negotiate or find a way to move out of the park.' Because, you know, there may be trouble with the police or something of that nature.

"And the reason I did that was, I felt that if I went down there and tried to relay that information, I'd be met with, 'Get out of here. You're not welcome here.' So that was the best way to relay information was through the public media ...

"And I advised some people in the office and some members of council what I'd heard."

Bernard: "I walked up to the fence line and I was kind of concerned about where my sister [Gina] was and my brother [Stacey, nicknamed "Burger"] ... and I said, 'Gina, be careful.' I was pretty nervous myself, watching, looking at all the cruisers on the outside of the area ... And part of why I went down there was to see if they needed anything and, you know, let them know we're still there with them." Then he left.

Stewart: "We were standing around in the – sandy area where the cars go down to the beach. We were standing there talking and this car comes down the road and pulls right up beside us and, here it's Gerald George [a band councillor, like Bernard and Bonnie]. He stops and says, 'What's going on, guys?'"

J.R.: "He was trying to be all buddy-buddy with us, trying to talk to us nice. But people at the time knew he was writing bad stuff about us, letters. And they were mad at him. And Stewart ..."

Stewart: "And I looked at him, like I couldn't believe it, because of what he had put in the paper about ... the guys that are staying in the army camp, and I don't, I don't know why he come down here after what he wrote in the paper ... I was angry.

"And I walked up to his car and asked him what he was doing around here. And he started to say something, so I give him a slap, and he took off, and then he stopped, and he turned around and looked back at me, and said, 'Worm, you're gonna get it!'

"So I threw a rock at him ... big enough to fit in the palm of my hand, or small enough ... I hit his car.

"After that, he took off, went up Army Camp Road ... And we went back to doing what we were doing, watching down the roads."

J.R.: "He stopped at the next police checkpoint. It was just down the road a little bit; you could see it. And you could see his mouth really flapping away at the cops. He was just there a couple of minutes. Then they sent him on his way."

Kevin: "[Bernard] come back again just before dark; that's when he brought the scanners and walkie-talkies and stuff ... I think he might have walked up that time [along the beach or through the bush on one of the deer trails], because I didn't see his truck around ...

"I had seen a scanner before and what they were for, so I started to get closer ... And the guy's got it working, and as soon as it turned on, it sounded pretty suspicious. And guys were whispering ...

"They were saying they had some badgers in the park and saying there's somebody on the roof. They're using code names or whatever. There was a lot of different stuff that they were saying on there, but it didn't really make no sense to me." ("Badgers" is the police term for "suspects." So they meant us, not themselves, in the park.)

Kevin: "I remember Dudley had been at the park store and was saying he couldn't see nobody up around that roof. I don't know if he had gone up on the roof or what. But everybody else kind of scattered out like, searching around."

Marlin: "And then we heard, like, they dispatched a TRU team – like a SWAT team. And we just felt something big was about to happen.

"So I jumped in my big ole Buick to spread the word ... and I went for a ride around the barracks to see if I could find anybody. And then I seen a dump truck up the road, up at Clifford's place, so I went up there because I knew my uncle Glenn was driving it, and I told him that stuff was going on down the park, and then I went back."

Glenn had come to seek Clifford's advice.

Clifford: "I was asked if they should give up. By that time, I knew that it would be useless to give up because, I call it 'the hit squad,' was there, and it would be dangerous for them to give up. And we are on rightful grounds there, I knew, because of the burial grounds."

PUNCH OUT

Cully: "I had been cooking, like, a meal in the kitchen, and I was going to tell the guys that the food was ready and ask them if they were going to come up or if they wanted me to bring it down there.

"It was dark out ... And I just went straight down the road [a gravel road inside the army camp, running parallel to Army Camp Road] and then I went through where the maintenance building is ... and I had a little bit of food with me, and I took it down there to give to Dudley and my son [J.R.] ... I thought they might be getting hungry by then ... So I pulled up and started asking where Dudley was ... And I believe it was Robert [Isaac] came over and said we needed help ... they needed more guys down there ... because something was happening ... When I looked, I seen, like a whole row of police ... They were shoulder to shoulder, coming up toward the fence.

"I said I would go to get help. One other girl said she would go to get help, and I asked her if she had a car, and she said she didn't ... So I told her to get in and [we drove up the road] and we were just kind of sitting there, and I'm like, where do I go looking for anybody ...

"But I seen lights coming along, and so I thought I would just sit there and wait and see if there was anybody going down to the park ... and it was the dump truck that went by, so I just decided to wait there because if it was somebody going to help, I didn't want to be in the way ... I wanted to keep the road clear for them."

Kevin: "After we had a look around, Bernard went down East Parkway Drive; maybe he had one of his brothers with him. And we noticed he was coming back ... and as he got closer you could hear him yell 'The police are coming.'"

Bernard: "They were dressed in – out of the normal gear. I realized they were riot police. That's the first time I've seen; I've only seen them on TV before. And they were carrying shields. The moonlight lit them up really well.

"My first thought was try to talk to them ... ask them to put their weapons away. That was one of the first things. To put their guns away. And I told them, our grandfathers are buried down here ... I said it loud enough so that they could hear me.

"No one responded to me ... Then, when I was speaking, it seemed like the pace turned into a faster pace. And I start backing up. And I spoke again; I told them to leave these people alone. And they just kept advancing, and so I backed up."

J.T.: "I seen three lines of cops coming down the road. They stretched from side to side. First row had shields and batons. There was a street light further down the road, past that first cottage, and that's how you could tell. Because they had to pass through that light."

Kevin: "They were basically shoulder to shoulder straight across the road and a few people deep. And they were marching.

"They were in full riot gear. They had their shields and their shields were touching each other so it was a solid line. And you could see the reflections off, like the plexiglass off their face shields of their helmets. And they had their batons, and they were using those to beat on their shields."

From the other side of the fence, some of us yelled at the police to get off our land.

Mike Cloud: "A lot of our guys kept reminding them that we have ... Native rights, this is a burial ground."

The police officers were wearing helmets equipped with remote audio to clearly receive orders. Still, two officers recorded in their notes later hearing "war cries" and "war yelps." A third noted having heard "a voice" saying that his grandfather was buried on this property, and it was Aboriginal land. In the Ipperwash Inquiry report, Justice Linden identified the voice as Bernard George's, when he was trying to reason with the OPP officers as they advanced. He also noted that, in that moment, Incident Commander John Carson's last orders – to clear the parking area outside the park fence – had been fulfilled. All of us were inside the park. But we had no idea that we were safe as long as we stayed on our side of the fence. No one had told us.

Stewart: "And they were accumulating there and, I can't remember how it started, but I remember I seen a guy walking a dog, so I went and got our dog; it was up where we were living [in one of the barracks]. And no sooner [had] I opened the door, he must have spotted the other dog, and he jumped out of the car and over the fence, and I was standing there when somebody said, 'Hey Worm, they kicked your dog' ... and I went over to the fence and I asked them, 'Who hit the dog?' Like 'Who hit the fucking dog?' And the cops come up to the fence, and I remember the one cop saying, 'Why? What are you going to do about it?' And he flicked his wrist and his night stick come out and swung at me. And I put my shoulder up, and he hit me across the shoulder there.

"So I looked, and I seen there was a pick-axe handle, and I said, 'give me that stick.' And I swung, and I hit him back ... He had a shield, he had a helmet on – the whole shebang ...

"I think that's when Bernard, I think that's when he come over the fence to try, try to reason with the police."

Leland: "I don't know if my dad went over the fence or if he stayed on our side. But somebody hit my dog, did something to it, and then he yelped. And then he said, 'who hit my dog?' And one of the officers said, 'I did. What are you going to do about it?' And then they clubbed my dad, so my dad clubbed him back ... And I put the dog on the bus. It was parked down the beach, and it was used kind of like a motor-home type of thing ... some of the seats were taken out and replaced with couches and beds. It was like a hangout for the young kids. So I stayed there, with the dog, so he wouldn't get hurt ... And I felt safer there, I guess."

Bernard: "Something took over me that night. Anger was in me for what they did to us all those years. The anger, it grew inside of me. I forgot about my kids, I forgot about [his wife] Roseanne." He grabbed a stick; possibly a length of pipe.

Stewart: "I heard him saying, something like 'these people are ...' I know he was saying something to them, and they grabbed a hold of him and started kicking the shit out of him.

"I was getting clubbed too and I could hear ... how hard they were hitting him, cause I've heard that sound before."

J.T.: "He was swinging around a staff, and he was telling them that this was our grandfather's land; you shouldn't be here. And the cops come rushing at him real fast, and he was swinging that staff around in a circle so they couldn't come near him, and the cops just flattened him with their shields. And they just start beating on him and, another line of cops come up and, like, they blocked him off and we couldn't get near him, and they were beating on him with their billy clubs and kicking at him when there's nothing we could do."

Bernard: "Once you grab me by the hair, I'm gonna fight ... I was fighting 'til they put me out."

Kevin: "He was holding his arm up to them, telling them to stop ... and I seen a club go up, and they clubbed him, and he went down, and then I heard them yell 'Punch out' or something like that." [This is an order for officers to yell and bang on their shields while rushing forward again and again on a group of people protesting or whatever. It's meant to intimidate them, making them retreat.]

J.R.: "They'd run at us real quick, bang on their shields, and then they'd back up again. Then they'd do it over again. I was scared." It kept us back.

Kevin: "[Bernard] was basically just laying on the ground getting clubbed ... You could see the clubs going up over the police officers' heads and going down – disappearing into the circle ... More than half a dozen."

Leland was still hiding in the bus with the family dog, watching out the window.

Leland: "I seen him being dragged and being kicked by officers ... I couldn't count them. Like ten; around there. I seen him from, like, the space in their legs."

Kevin: "I remember Gina, she was yelling that was her brother out there, and 'you got to do something, they're, they're gonna kill him.'"

Gina: "I stood there ten feet away and watched a thousand – I don't know how many, but to me it was a thousand cops, and they grabbed my brother. They just rushed him and grabbed him and pulled him onto the road, and they beat him right in front of us, and I said: 'They're gonna kill my brother!' – and they almost did. And that's when we rushed out with the bus."

DUDLEY GEORGE SHOT

Abe's grandson, Nicholas, got the bus going, steered it toward the gate and hit the gas a bit more, pushing the bus against the dumpster we had manhandled into place there earlier to keep the police out.

J.T.: "And the bus went forward again, and it stalled out. And when Nick started [it] up, the bus, it backfired."

Leland: "[The dumpster] got smashed out of the way ... [and the bus kept going] like at a fast walk ... [We were going] to try to help Slippery [Bernard] ... get up as close as we can to him, and probably bring him on the bus ... And there was smashing and stuff ... and cops trying to get in the back window, like the emergency door window, near the floor. And there was a laundry basket in there, and I was trying to plug the window with it so they couldn't get in ... and the dog was barking at them ... and things banging on the side of the bus, and yelling and, like, gunshots ... And the bus was going forward ... and then it was going backward."

J.T.: "And shortly after the bus backfired, that's when the cops started shooting at us ... It was like a pop, then it was just like how you watch movies and stuff and see like an automatic gun go off ... and it sounded like that; it was just constantly fire."

Kevin: "And I seen [Bernard] being dragged. There wasn't as much of a beating going on, but I could see that he was still being clubbed as they were dragging him away ... He wasn't moving; he was just getting dragged ... And the bus was still trying to make it in that direction ... As I followed the bus out, it made it out onto the paved part ... right at the end of Army Camp Road.

"It must have been right at that time when I heard the first shots ... It started kind of slow, couple of quick pops ... and the bus started to come back, and I heard those first shots fired. And then it was just a matter of seconds and there was a whole volley of them ... There was quite a number of muzzle flashes ... The ones [the OPP officers] that were further down by the bus, there was quite a number of them too were firing ... And I looked back at the main crowd of people, and I seen a lot of them were basically running, ducking, trying to take cover of some sort ... and you could see the ground would be getting kicked up around in amongst those people."

Gina: "I looked at my cousin J.R., and it was like fireflies because there were so many all over the place ... Until – we were standing beside a sign and I heard ting, ting. Those were bullets hitting the sign, and I went, 'Holy fuck, J.R' and that's when we both hit the ground."

Leland: "And Nug [Nicholas], he said he got hit ... like, by a bullet. And there was a kind of grinding sound ... And I was, like, on my knees looking out the window ... And I kind of, I seen Dudley laying there on the ground. And his shirt was bloody, and I knew he was shot."

Kevin: "When the bus had gone by me, that's when I heard somebody [Stacey, Bernard's brother] yell out that Dudley had been hit. Dudley was shot ... So I basically started walking toward where I'd heard that Dudley had been shot. And I seen the form of somebody lying there.

"The bus, it was having trouble getting back in there. The dumpster was still kind of in the road. It hit it [the dumpster] maybe once or twice, trying to reverse to make it back in. And there was fairly loose sand there, so it ... was having to, it wasn't able to push it [the dumpster] out of the way like it did when it came out.

"There was people that were pushing the dumpster out of the way, and I made my way over to Dudley. I seen it was Dudley, and there was quite a bit of blood around his shirt, on top of his chest area. His shirt was pretty much soaked.

"I knelt down to him and grabbed his hand, like, basically give him a handshake ... I heard him try to say something, but I knew he couldn't talk. He was bleeding pretty good. So, basically, I told him he did a good job in fighting out there.

"And it might have been someone ... and J.T., I think, I'm not sure if he helped carry Dudley back in ... Once the bus had made it in, we followed, carried Dudley in ... And I heard someone say something about get the 'OPP Who' car [the old rez car with this painted on the side] ... and we put Dudley in the back."

J.T.: "I went running out there, and Stewart George and Roderick George and ... they're picking him up and taking him back in the park."

J.R.: "I couldn't even get a hold of one of his legs to help them get him in the car, there were so many people that wanted to help him."

J.T.: "And they got him in the back of the 'OPP Who' car. I think Stewart George was in the front seat with Robert Isaac, and I was in the back seat with Dudley. I was putting pressure on his wound as we went up to the front, the barracks. I was scared for Dudley ... He looked at me, and he smiled and was just gasping."

Gina: "I remember us picking him up off the ground, and it was J.T. that got in the car too. He was just a little kid trying his best to help." They raced up the gravel road that ran beside Army Camp Road, others following in cars and on foot.

Pierre: "They brought Dudley up and said, 'Hey Pierre, put him in your car; take him to the hospital.' But it had no plates on it. No insurance, nothing."

Cully: "By the time we got up there, there was a bunch of people around the gate, but I couldn't get close. There were too many people. So I just hopped out of the car, and I went running over, and that's when they told me Dudley had been shot." By then, people had put Dudley in the back seat of Pierre's big white rez car; J.T. was with him in the back, pressing his sweater against where the blood was coming out.

"And I says, alright, you keep the pressure on, and I'm jumping in the front seat."

J.T.: "They told me to keep talking to him and make sure he's – he stays awake and keeps conscious."

Marcia: "When I heard that Dudley was shot, I was just panicking and wanting to find my sons. I started driving down there. And there was a whole line of lights coming. And one of the cars was Marlin, and his face was just ashen, and he says, 'Don't go down there. The cops have shot up everything.' So I reluctantly turned around, even though I still hadn't seen Kevin. But I had my mum [Melva] with me ..."

"When we got back to the gate area, we saw our cousin Roderick sort of staggering around. I heard him say, 'He's got a hole in him.' And I noticed Pierre's car wasn't there anymore, and I looked in at [Roderick's] son [Nicholas]; he was huddled in the back of the car. And I just got back in my car, and I was determined to go to the nearest payphone and call for ambulances for whoever was shot ... I was fearful that my younger son [Kevin] was also shot and lying somewhere. I didn't know; no one could reassure me that he was okay ...

"So I went out of the gate. I made sure that I stopped and signalled and remained within the speed limit. I didn't want anyone to come chasing after me."

Marlin: "Everybody was kind of just standing around. We were, like, figuring out what – what happened, and who was all gone, who was all missing. We had a head count, and everybody was just kind of walking around."

Glenn: "We stayed by the fire [in the park]. We burned tobacco, and I remember Elwood was cooking some hamburgers up and thought maybe somebody would eat, but I don't know if anybody ate ... And for some reason I had this feeling [come] over me that I had to go and check on something. I didn't know what. And when I got to the front [gate], the first thing, 'Where's my Mum [Melva]?' That's what went through my mind was 'Where's my Mum?'"

CHAPTER TEN

After the Shooting

He had been hit and was hurting badly, but Nicholas managed to keep backing up the bus 'til he got it inside the park fence again. Outside it, Crowd Management Unit leader Wade Lacroix watched this happen. When it was done, he ordered a cease-fire, called all officers together, and immediately asked for a casualty report. When he got it, "no casualties," he ordered a recount, telling them to check the ditches too.

He told the Ipperwash Inquiry ten years later: "They say they've got everybody. I have a hard time believing that. I tell them to do it again, just because of the amount of violence, the amount of action that had taken place."

There were no casualties among the nearly forty OPP officers deployed that night. No broken bones or serious injuries either. One officer had a strained knee ligament and a twisted ankle, but that was it.[1]

Lacroix then ordered his officers to resume their box formation and, at a "high trot" pace, return to the command centre down East Parkway Drive. There, he asked any who had fired his weapon to step forward. Six officers acknowledged they had discharged their weapons.

At around the same time, Sergeant Mark Wright sent two detective constables to the Strathroy Hospital to arrest a male (later identified as Nicholas Cottrelle) due to arrive there with a gunshot wound. He was to be arrested for attempted murder. A few minutes later, a report came in about a white car with a flat tire arriving at a house on Nauvoo

Road. Someone in the car had been shot and needed medical care; they had subsequently left the area. At 11:40 p.m., Wright instructed Detective Sergeant Richardson to find the car and arrest the occupants for attempted murder. He also sent more officers to the hospital.

On arrival, the police said they were there to ensure the safety of patients and staff. There was a rumour that First Nations people might attack the hospital or be disruptive. They set up a communications centre in the patient registration area, and officers, in what looked to the staff like full riot gear, patrolled the halls.

One of the two women doctors on duty that night, Dr. Saettler, found it distracting and intimidating. She also felt "that degree of police presence was excessive ... sort of fear mongering on the part of the police to justify their presence there."

The first patient to arrive was Nicholas Cottrelle. He was taken to the trauma room. They found a round wound about a centimetre in diameter on the right side of his lower back and a four-inch linear abrasion on his right side. X-rays of his chest and abdomen were ordered.

Bernard George was wheeled in about five minutes later. Nicholas didn't recognize him at first, he was so badly beaten. Staff immediately focused on Bernard.

He had been delayed getting to the hospital that night because the ambulance in which he was being transported had travelled a good portion of the way at the regulation eighty kilometres an hour. It was driven by a new St. John Ambulance volunteer, Glen Morgan, while another volunteer, Karen Bakker-Stephens, a first-year nursing student at a local community college, tried to keep Bernard from losing consciousness. The two volunteers had been sent to Ipperwash Park that evening to operate the radio, telephone, computer, and other equipment in the St. John Ambulance communications vehicle that Incident Commander John Carson had ordered. It had the St. John Ambulance logo on the side, but it was a utility vehicle. The only reason an operating ambulance was there at all had been to transport the two volunteers to the job. But it was a minimally equipped one, lacking even a blood pressure cuff.

Karen Bakker-Stephens checked Bernard's vital signs every ten minutes and, for a second time, he seemed to lose consciousness. This time, she could not find a pulse. He didn't seem to be breathing at all, and his pupils appeared unresponsive to her flashlight. She asked Morgan to initiate Code 4 and, upon receiving the okay to do this, the car sped up to the 110–115 km/h range. She shook Bernard, telling him to wake up. She worried he had a brain injury. She thought it was life threatening.

At the hospital, Dr. Saettler saw lacerations on Bernard's scalp, a deep cut on his lip, and bruises on his forehead, chest, and forearm. Bernard continued to slip in and out of consciousness. Dr. Saettler noted that "he didn't know where he was and wasn't responding appropriately to questions."

Staff stabilized his neck and back. X-rays and blood work were also ordered; there was no alcohol in his blood.

Dr. Saettler asked Nicholas for some background. At first, he wouldn't speak to her ("They might not have a level of trust that would allow them to volunteer information," Dr. Saettler said later). But eventually, he explained that Bernard had been beaten by maybe nine police officers and kicked in the abdomen.

The doctors noted extensive bruising on Bernard's whole body, as well as his outer forearm, consistent with someone raising an arm to ward off blows. It appeared to Dr. Marr, another doctor on duty that night who prepared the report on Bernard's condition, that he had been hit "quite hard many times with a blunt object." The bruises, many of which were linear and elongated, "seemed consistent with the history of his being beaten with a baton." Bernard George had "received multiple blunt wounds to the head, face, chest, abdomen and limbs."

Another hospital physician also noted an absence of metacarpal fractures, also known as boxer's fractures, on Bernard's hands. If present, she told the OPP's Special Investigations Unit that subsequently investigated the events of that night, it would suggest "a fistfight where he was at least an equal participant or ... had thrown some punches." From the evidence, Bernard had not managed even that.

Dr. Marr's report recorded twenty-eight areas of tenderness, each representing a separate application of force; some might have been from the kick of a boot.

He had multiple soft tissue injuries, again considered consistent with a severe beating, and severe head trauma as well.

Both attending physicians wanted Bernard sent to a larger hospital for a CT scan and other tests. This did not happen.

Bernard woke up to see police officers on both sides of his bed. One told him that he was under arrest for attempted murder. Less than two days later, the OPP took him to the Sarnia jail, overriding the doctors' recommended follow-up.

RACE TO THE HOSPITAL

Dudley George was the last person to arrive at the hospital that night, delayed by a flat tire.

Pierre had been going as fast as his old Chevrolet Impala (bought for fifty dollars) could go when a tire blew. He turned in at the next driveway, the farm of Hank and Mary Veens, and Cully jumped out. Mr. Veens was already heading downstairs when Cully started banging on the door. He had been woken by the thump, thump, thumping sound coming down the road.

Cully: "He was very helpful. He got right on the phone ... He had to call upstairs for his wife to because she was the one that knew what [number to call]." Mrs. Veens came downstairs and packaged up some fresh tea towels and ice for Dudley.

"And we went out to the road and sat there and waited ... And I kept reminding J.T. to keep the pressure on ... It seemed like forever, but I think it was probably only about five minutes ... It was almost like we realized that no one was coming to help. And Dudley was just going to die if we sat there. So we decided to go ahead to at least try and get there. Flat tire or not."

From the back seat, she could hear J.T. telling Dudley: "It's going to be okay. You're going to be okay. We're soon going to be at the hospital. Everything's going to be okay."

J.T.: "He was still conscious. He was still breathing. He was, like, panting; his breathing was getting real heavy and deep."

At 11:55 p.m., Constable Tracy Dobbin and her partner were dispatched to Strathroy Hospital to arrest "a carload of Natives" en route there in a white car with a flat tire. A request was also sent to the OPP's Chatham Communications Centre asking about any reports of a stolen vehicle, with the officer saying: "We can't find this white car. White car with a flat tire. It hasn't been spotted on its way to the hospital yet ... So they may be trying to boost another vehicle."

Then it was spotted, coming into Strathroy. Sparks were flying off the rim of the wheel.

Cully noticed the police cars following them, but that's all. Pierre drove right up to the Emergency entrance of the hospital.

Cully: "We hopped out. There was an attendant standing by the door, and I said, 'Bring a stretcher.' I turned around to get the back door opened, and the attendant was still standing there. I said, 'Bring a fucking stretcher.' I seen the police nod his head. He was right up by the hospital doors, and once he nodded his head, I noticed the attendant started to move – and that's when they [the police] grabbed me ...

"They grabbed my arms and put them behind my back and put me right down on the ground. My face went right through some shrubs, and I got my glasses knocked off. And I was trying to ask them to let me see my brother ... And I could see that Pierre was held up against the wall, the cement wall and, like, his face was right up against it. And Pierre was asking what they were doing, and they said we were under arrest for attempted murder."

She and Pierre were handcuffed and taken away in an OPP cruiser.

"I never seen Dudley after that."

J.T.: "When we got to the hospital, they pulled Pierre out, and they arrested him on the cement. They pulled Cully out of the car ... and they had her on the ground, and they arrested her and put them in cruisers and took them away, and then I was in the back of the car. I was, like, trying to help Dudley and ... there was cops sort of like opened up both doors and they were dragging me away from Dudley, and they tried to arrest me, and I was squirming around on the ground, and I got away from them.

"I got back to the car, and I was trying to help Dudley ... And the cops got a hold of me, and they handcuffed me, and they took me and put me in the back of the cruiser ... I was trying to kick at the door and kick at him ... and they put a strap around my feet so I couldn't kick nothing ... They said that I was going to be arrested for mischief, assault on a police officer, and conspiracy – for attempted murder, like, part of a murder."

At 12:05 a.m., OPP Chief Superintendent Parkin ordered Pierre's car seized. He also wanted enough police kept on at the hospital "in case a bunch of Indians go over there and go crazy."

Dudley was wheeled into the trauma room, and hospital staff spent twenty minutes working on him. At 12:20 a.m., they gave up attempts to resuscitate him. One doctor thought he might have been dead on arrival. Still, she felt it would have helped if she could have talked to Cully and Pierre.

The autopsy found that a lethally powerful bullet had entered Dudley's body above the left collarbone, breaking it. It travelled from left to right through his lungs, fracturing one rib, piercing another, tearing a pulmonary artery, and eventually lodged in soft tissue in his back. The broken blood vessels caused internal bleeding, bringing on shock and death.

The review of the autopsy said that Cully, Pierre, and J.T. had provided appropriate medical care under the circumstances, including their decision to try to get to the hospital rather than wait for an ambulance that never was seen.

At 3:22 a.m., Dudley was placed in a private room. An OPP constable came in and tested his hands for gunshot residue (which came back negative). The constable then photographed Dudley's body and took away his clothes.

By this time, another of Dudley's brothers, Sam (Maynard), and another sister, Pam, were at the hospital. They wanted permission to smudge Dudley's body, "to start that cleansing process for the body, to help that spirit, now that it was going to start to prepare itself to make that journey back to the spirit world," as Sam subsequently explained it to the Ipperwash Inquiry.

THE TELEPHONE BOOTH

Marcia Simon had gone in the opposite direction that night. Once she got to the intersection of Army Camp Road and Highway 21, she signalled and turned left up the highway. She was headed for Mac-Pherson's Restaurant some four kilometres away; it had a telephone booth outside. Partway there, police cruisers came chasing, lights flashing, sirens going. One pulled up beside her, then pulled back.

"I had mixed feelings about turning to them for help, since they had just shot up our people ... The other thought I had was they'll see I'm not trying to run away ... [when I stop at MacPherson's].

"My mother was really scared with all those guns pointed at us. So I told her to duck down. The police were in the ditch with shotguns pointed at us just as I was turning the corner [toward the restaurant]."

She got to the phone, dialed 0, and when the operator came on, "I told her, 'we need ambulances and you need to let the media know. Our people have been shot up at Stoney Point, and they're going to shoot me too.' The operator said that she would notify the police, and I said: 'it was the police that was trying to shoot us.' Because by then they were out of their cruisers, standing behind them with shotguns levelled at me ...

"And they told me to get away from the phone. And I told them I was only trying to get medical help. I was worried about my son. I needed help. *We* needed help ... They kept advancing. They hid behind the gas pumps with shotguns levelled and kept advancing.

"I turned my back to them ... Not too long after that, I had the phone violently jerked from me, and I remember meeting the hood of my car and the ground. And I could hear my mother yelling in the background. She was trying to tell them about the bone graft [on her wrist] I had just had, and it was healing, and they paid no attention. I remember being handcuffed with an officer on my back, with those plastic cuffs, and cutting off circulation in my hands ... My glasses were knocked off and just lying in the parking lot. And they even got into my purse, and they were throwing things all over the parking lot. I couldn't get over them throwing my stuff all over that parking lot. And I told them that wasn't necessary ...

"My mother was down on the ground trying to pray. She had her medicines with her, and they had shotguns levelled right at her head, yelling at her to put her hands in the air. And she was pleading that she couldn't because she had arthritis ...

"And I pleaded with them, leave her alone ... I asked them if that's how they were trained to treat old, grey-haired widows, and they seemed to calm down a little."

They wanted to send Melva home.

"I told them to take her home to Kettle Point because she had telephone service there, so she could make calls." Marcia asked her to call her department head at school (H.B. Beal, in London) – "to arrange a supply teacher for me. We're supposed to do that ourselves if we can't make it into work."

Marcia was taken to the garage part of the OPP headquarters in Forest. They took a mug shot, took away some of her clothes, plus her shoes and socks. Then they put her in a cell. "There was a mattress and an old grey wool blanket and it just looked filthy. Just the idea that there were these other criminals that had been in there before. People who knew me wouldn't expect me to be in jail ... It just felt, these guys don't even know that I'm a respected school teacher. Same as my mum: She's a respected elder in the community. To be treated like that!"

At 2:00 a.m. or so, a woman in a red dress came by and asked if Marcia had made a phone call. No, they had not let her do that. They had not read her her rights either.

In the end, they released her, but into the custody of the Anishi-naabek Kettle Point police, who brought her back to Kettle Point.

THE POLICE ROADBLOCK

By then, a bunch of people had gathered at the mall near the turnoff to Kettle Point from Highway 21; they had a big fire going by the road. Band council chief Tom Bressette had already called John Carson at the command post. At 1:30 in the morning, he headed into Forest seeking an update on Bernard; there were rumours that he had been shot too. He was stopped by a police roadblock.

Tom: "They got a gun pointed at your head ... You can tell you're goin' to be shot by how many bullets [red laser target lights] are on you. And they're all over your face and your head. That's what they're focused on, all pointing at you, at the roadblock. I had to go through three of them. The second one, I very near got shot.

"'What you got in your hand?' I had to freeze. 'It's a phone.' I had to put it down where he could see it."

At 2:54 a.m., Tom Bressette called Carson back because Bonnie Bressette had come to the mall and was volunteering to drive over to the army base to speak to the people there; to see if there were any women and children who wanted to come away. Carson told him to give the former chief his phone number as reference.

Bonnie: "It was the worst night of my life." Her daughter Gail insisted on coming with her, and they drove into the sudden white glare of multiple spotlights and police.

"When those police stood there with those guns pointed at us, and there was not another soul around anyplace, I was never so scared in my whole life.

"Anyway, I gave them [Carson's] number, and they backed off."

At 4:54 a.m., Bonnie called Carson herself. The people occupying the park and living in the army base wanted assurance that the OPP would not come in and forcibly remove them. Carson told her he gave them his word.

Bonnie: "All I can recall is telling whoever was down there when I went back again was, there was going to be nobody coming in to attack them."

BACK AT THE PARK

Down at the beach, the Ipperwash Park store was on fire.

Glenn: "I remember hearing them say, 'Torch it' when we heard Dudley was pronounced dead. That's what I heard ... I think I was trying to use the phone, because I was trying to find out where my mum [Melva] was ... If I had enough arms and legs, I would have probably burnt the building down too. But I was too busy."

Marlin: "And we were checking out the bus and we were checking out Waldo's car and, like, holy smokes!" Warren ("Waldo") George had driven out the gate behind the bus earlier. "There was a whole bunch of dents all over his hood and bullet holes in his doorway ... and his window was shot out ...

"We start looking around where everything happened at, and we seen like, there's blood spots on the road where Dudley got shot ... where he must have fell down the first time ... and more blood spots over there, over by the dumpster. There was bullet casings all over the place ... Handfuls and handfuls."

He put one in his pocket. When the OPP Special Investigations Unit finally cordoned the area off with yellow tape (not until September 18) and began investigating it as a possible crime scene, he handed it over to one of the investigating officers.

Kevin found himself at the OPP's Tactical Operations Centre site in the Ministry of Natural Resources parking lot off East Parkway Drive.

Kevin: "I had gone down there to see for myself what was down there. They were talking about these ambulances that were around to help our people and stuff like that. What I witnessed there, the St. John Ambulance, yeah, they were there, [but] it wasn't no ambulance. It was full of computer stuff. It was like a command centre for the police. It was marked St. John Ambulance. And I had a look inside, and that's where I seen all that equipment. And there was nothing that I seen that resembled anything that would help with injuries."

When he headed back to the barracks, Bonnie was there.

"She was there asking to take – offering to take out a lot of ... women and children. I was one of the people that spoke up to say, 'You going to go out there into the cops? They're the ones that are killing people' ... I also heard at that time that my mother and my grandma were missing. And we'd heard that Slippery [Bernard] had been shot ... And all kinds of things were being said. We didn't really know what to think ... and I didn't know what to do, so I decided the best thing was, I go try to rest, seeing as it was getting morning time ...

"I must have crashed out for about two hours – I guess part of the reason it helped me sleep was I had asked, basically asked the Creator that we be shown some support and people would come. And when I woke up, there was quite a number – I'd say easily a thousand already gathered around that gatehouse and more coming down the road from Kettle Point ... There was people everywhere that were basically supporting us – what I had asked for."

Stewart: "When I seen all those people coming down the road, I remember feeling that I was going to live ... [In his mind, there was] no telling but they were going to come back and finish the rest of us guys."

By that time too, however, the media had received a press release that Incident Commander John Carson had prepared. It said in part:

> A private citizen's vehicle was damaged by a number of First Nations people armed with baseball bats. As a result of this, the OPP Crowd Management Team was deployed to disperse the crowd of First Nations people which had gathered at that location ... As the Crowd Management Unit was leaving the area, a school bus and a full sized vehicle drove through the Provincial Park fence striking a dumpster, then pushing the dumpster and the vehicles into the Crowd Management Team. Occupants of those two vehicles fired upon police officers and subsequently police officers returned fire.[2]

The release was issued at 6:09 a.m. on September 7, between the time the Special Investigations Unit was dispatched and when it arrived at the command centre, placing a media embargo on Carson. It was only at the Ipperwash Inquiry that the inaccuracies and falsehoods in the press release were finally brought to light. Meanwhile, as Justice Linden wrote in his Ipperwash Inquiry report, "It no doubt had the effect of portraying the occupiers in a violent light to all who read the press release." In fact, the police had fired on unarmed Nishnaabe men, women, and children.

Later that day, Bonnie was included in a meeting with band council chief Tom Bressette, senior OPP officials, and Ovide Mercredi, national chief of the Assembly of First Nations, who had come down from Ottawa. Together, they drafted a plan for defusing the situation. The police agreed to pull back their roadblocks and generally reduce their presence. Bruce Elijah and Bob Antone brought in thirty-six Oneida Long House peacekeepers who set up checkpoints around the perimeter of our territory, the former army camp, adding to and relieving some of our men who had been doing this since July. Healers arrived to smudge and provide counselling.

Cully: "We were all individually checked out by a shaman to make sure there was no bad stuff on us. Everybody that was involved went through that. And it gave you a sense of peacefulness and calmness."

MEMORANDUM OF UNDERSTANDING

A week later, Minister of Indian Affairs Ron Irwin accepted Tom Bressette's invitation to come and talk.[3] He arrived at Kettle Point on September 13 with a draft memorandum of understanding on how the federal government and the First Nation would proceed and presented this to the chief and band council. It first proposed that the federal government appoint a negotiator directly responsible to the minister of Indian Affairs within one week. This negotiator was to be acceptable to the First Nation. Item two said "that the Federal Government is committed to transferring the land in dispute, namely former Camp Ipperwash ... to the First Nation as reserve land."[4] Other items dealt with responsibility for environmental cleanup of the former army camp, honouring the burial grounds there, and funding a healing process for the community.

Tom Bressette: "When I think back now about the memorandum of understanding that we had to deal with, Mr. Irwin was a – he was a pretty fast talker and he, all he wanted to do was, he kept saying 'Do you want to make a deal? You want to make a deal?' And he was impressing on council he was there from the government trying to resolve matters. There was a lot of pressure in the community to find some way to resolve what was going on. And we had a tremendous amount of people waiting in the community centre while we were meeting with the federal government ... We didn't even have a debriefing session ... or even the opportunity to even take a breath. It was all push, push, push. And I don't think it was fair for them to come and deal with us that way at that particular time and walk away with a document, saying, 'This is it.'

"They appointed someone, but I don't think he was mutually acceptable. They just told us who our negotiator was."

There was no mention of time in the agreement; no dates and deadlines for completing negotiations on the return of the land or for cleaning it up. There was no mention of restoring the land as Reserve #43: the Stoney Point Reserve.

Ten years later, when the Ipperwash Inquiry was finally underway, the land had not yet been returned to the reserve. Nor had the cleanup of unexploded munitions begun. It took a strong recommendation from that Inquiry to move things forward again. Meanwhile, the government had quietly resumed control of the army base. In addition to the contracts issued to the Kettle Point band office for mowing the lawns and maintenance, they added one for providing security at the gate.

A week after the minister of Indian Affairs brought his ready-to-sign memorandum of understanding to the Kettle and Stony Point chief and council, on September 18, Bonnie Bressette was driving past the corner of Army Camp Road and East Parkway when she noticed what looked like police crime-scene tape around the area where Dudley had been shot. She stopped to have a look.

"And when I seen all of them, they're all crawling along the ground close together, I asked the one man that seemed to be the head of the investigation, I asked what they were looking for, because I didn't see how they could find anything there for the simple fact there had been hundreds of people that had been down there since Dudley died ... That should have been all roped off, but it wasn't; that's what really bothered me."

Charges Laid Against Us

Twenty-four of us who had been involved in taking back the park and our ancestral burial grounds were charged. The charges were mostly for small things like forcible entry, unauthorized entry, interference with the lawful use or enjoyment of property, or mischief, but also for assault ... Almost all of these charges were subsequently dropped on the grounds of colour of right, the reasonable justification for what would otherwise be trespassing that had been raised repeatedly at Toronto meetings on September 5 and 6.

Bernard George was acquitted (a "directed verdict") of the assault charges against him when the Crown was unable to substantiate them.

The judge also acquitted young Nicholas Cottrelle, charged with dangerous driving and assaulting a police officer with a weapon (the school bus), believing the evidence that he was on a rescue mission.

Warren ("Waldo") George, who drove the car behind the bus that night and who actually hit at least one OPP officer, was charged with criminal negligence in the operation of a motor vehicle and assaulting a police officer with a weapon (the car). He was convicted and sent to jail for six months. And his driver's licence was taken away for two years.

The OPP officer who killed Dudley with that fatal shot never went to jail. Kenneth ("Tex") Deanne, second-in-command of the Tactics and Rescue Unit that night, was found guilty of criminal negligence causing death but given a conditional sentence of two years less one day to be served in the community. Even then, he appealed the verdict, with support from the police association. But both his appeals, first to the Ontario Court of Appeal and then to the Supreme Court of Canada were unsuccessful.

Two Boats Travelling Side by Side

It was hard after Dudley died.

Cully: "I tried going back to work [as a custodian at the school in Forest], and they were just atrocious. There might have been three that would even talk to me. They didn't like it that us Natives had gotten our land back; that we were allowed to stay here."

Marcia: "I tried to carry on working ... There's supposed to be a system [in the public school system] that kicks in whenever a tragic event happens, to provide support to the people affected. And that was turned down for us. We were denied the services of counselling and support ... And we weren't supposed to even talk about it, and yet I had my students coming to the door concerned about my well-being. They'd seen on the news where I'd been put in jail, and they were horrified ... I resigned [at the end of the school year]."

When we heard that the OPP had all received counselling, that bothered us. It bothered us that they were seen as doing what they had to do, and our peacekeepers, our nation builders, our warriors, were seen as terrorists, as troublemakers – or "animals" and "jerks," like Gerald George from Kettle Point had written in the paper.

What happened at Kettle Point was hard too. Our culture was banned at the school. A kid was sent home for wearing moccasins. When someone tried to smudge the band office one day, she was told to stop; told they hadn't developed a policy on smudging yet.

Cully: "The Christians against the traditional Indians. That's on *every* reserve, and the Christians gotta have *their* way."

Someone scratched out the luminescent paint on the word "Stony" on the sign outside the band office, so the word Stony disappeared at night.

Cully: "Still, there was a sense of comfort being here, because we had this fence. The cops can't come running right in after us with their guns ...

"One time I stepped out the door [of the barracks where I'm still living]. I was going over to Glenny's. I had a white T-shirt on, and I was turning to go down the steps, and all of a sudden I felt like I was a target! Can they really see me in this white shirt? They must be in the corn field over there. I turned around, come back in the house. I got a dark shirt on, and then I went out the other door and come around. I felt they were *there*."

Pierre: "I've got posttraumatic, eh? I live that [night] 24/7. That's my job."

Having to go to court tied up a lot of us for a long time; years, in fact, because they kept putting the cases over, or most of them. There were forty-three charges. And we would all have to show up every time there was a court date because if we weren't there when our name was called, we could be convicted. Some of us didn't have cars or just had rez cars you couldn't take out on the road.

Kevin: "That actually helped build the community, everyone having those court dates together."

Marcia: "There'd always be a convoy of Stoney Pointers going to the courthouse – with placards too, of course!"

Kevin: "And we'd have time to talk, what was goin' on. And if it was wintertime and you needed help with plowing, somebody would say, 'alright.'"

Some of the younger people organized a summer music festival in the former Ipperwash Provincial Park. They called it the Aazhoodena Jamboree. Kevin got a group of us together and we dismantled the cedar walls in one of the barracks to build a stage for the performers, sharing all the work; it wasn't easy pulling all those nails out of that old cedar without splitting it either. We put together a gazebo kind of thing, with a roof in case it rained.

But one day, a crew from the Ministry of Natural Resources turned up. They said they were only removing ministry infrastructure, but they took out the bandstand. Destroyed it completely.

Kevin: "I think the reason why is because we were building not just our community, but our nation. We had people from Walpole, Sarnia,

Munsee, Chippewas on the Thames. For three or four years, they'd come here, they'd sing, they'd smudge, drum."

Maynard ("Sam") George hadn't really been part of all we had been doing to get our land back. But when Dudley was shot by that OPP officer, he made it his business to ensure that the whole truth of who and what had killed his little brother was brought to public light. With his wife, Veronica, his sister Pam, and some of us, he pulled together a team. He hired lawyers (many of them worked pro bono), and he started calling for a public inquiry. He contacted all the groups that had been supporting us: union groups, church groups. He spoke to them and to other Nishnaabe activist groups and the Assembly of First Nations, getting support from all over. People organized marches and demonstrations. Some of us made banners and marched too. And he encouraged different groups to hold their own events too.

One of these was a fundraiser at Convocation Hall at the University of Toronto. It was organized by the Elementary Teachers' Federation of Ontario and held on March 1, 2002. The list of speakers and performers included Elder Lilian Pikawankwaat, who offered the opening prayer; Nimkey Az zawan, who led a drumming circle offering an Honour Song; Murray Klippenstein, the George family lawyer; Cree/Métis actor/filmmaker Tantoo Cardinal; Odawa playwright Alanis King; dub poet Lillian Allen; singer Sylvia Tyson; and Wayne Samuelson, president of the Ontario Federation of Labour.

By then, the number of organizations calling for an inquiry, and often also contributing money to support the cause, was over a hundred. They were churches, unions, and social and racial justice groups. There were also Ontario city councils, the United Nations Human Rights Committee, plus many Indigenous organizations, including the Union of Ontario Indians. Sam and his lawyer team also launched a civil suit against the Ontario government for the wrongful death of Dudley. This helped bring the demand for an inquiry into the political arena, especially leading up to the next provincial election. Liberal leader Dalton McGuinty promised that if he was elected, he would order a public inquiry. It was understood that if this happened, the lawsuit would be dropped.

In November 2003, newly elected Premier McGuinty honoured his promise. He drafted an order-in-council to mandate an inquiry into the shooting death of Dudley George.

The first part of the mandate was only to examine the events surrounding Dudley's death that day in 1995. The second part was "to make recommendations directed to the avoidance of violence in similar circumstances." This meant it could look into the history behind that violence. And that's what the man appointed to head the Inquiry, Justice Sidney B. Linden, did.

It was hard going through that Inquiry. We had to show up as witnesses; they could even issue a summons to make us come. Once there, we had to remember. We had to talk about that night when Dudley was killed. And we had to sit there being grilled by all the lawyers that were out to discredit us. There was one for the OPP, one for the police association, another for Mike Harris, and a couple of others. When Kevin was being interrogated – and that went on for three days – the lawyer representing the George family challenged the police association's lawyer for being improper. He said his tone was improper because he kept trying to trip Kevin up. Twice, Justice Linden intervened to get those lawyers to back off.

Marcia: "When they had my mother up there to interview, they played the tape from that night [Marcia's call to the telephone operator, which was recorded] and all the family heard her screaming and crying. You could hear them crying all over that auditorium. That was awful."

When Bonnie was on the witness stand, she told them bluntly: "There's one thing the Commission here does not understand, you don't see very many of our people out at these hearings because nobody wants to relive it."

Still, the Inquiry was worthwhile; at least it got things moving again on the return of our land. One of its recommendations said: "The federal government should *immediately* return the former army camp to the peoples of the Kettle Point and Stony Point First Nation, and guarantee that it will assume complete responsibility for an appropriate environmental clean-up of the site."

The recommendation said "the peoples," not the band council. But Tom Bressette was still the chief of the Kettle and Stony Point band council. He had become a regional chief of the Assembly of First Nations by then too. We [Stoney Pointers] were consulted but not given a big say in what went on. For us, it was pretty simple: give us back our homeland. But the negotiations around actually doing it and how it would be done went on for years. A lot of it happened in Ottawa as well, where a consulting firm, Ishkonigan Consulting and Mediation, was involved. It was founded and run by Phil Fontaine, former national chief of the Assembly of First Nations.

A final settlement agreement was announced by the federal government in February 2016. It ran on for nearly a hundred pages, though many of us never saw the whole thing. A short summary was made available for everyone to read. Then it was voted on by the Kettle and Stony Point band council and signed, and there was a big celebration around it at Kettle Point attended by the federal minister of Indigenous and Northern Affairs and the minister of National Defence and a bunch of others from Ottawa. Supposedly, the land was returned at that point. But the federal government kept control of it. They would keep control, they said, until the cleanup of all the unexploded ordnances and environmental toxins was complete. Meanwhile, they had also built their control into the final settlement agreement. Because all those pages of clauses and subclauses made all the actions on the land, from "Archaeological and Cultural Considerations" like our burial grounds to "Land Use Plan" like rebuilding houses and the community, subject to federal laws plus bureaucratic policies and procedures – complete with the government's own "dispute-resolution" mechanism.

There was no time frame committing the government to completing the cleanup by a certain date either. It was understood the process might take twenty years. Even more.

Four years on, very little had been done.

Bonnie: "They have dragged this on for *so* long. They've had contracts with I think three different people, and then they start all over. They haven't even finished the investigation."

Kevin: "They're procrastinating, DND; that sucks ... There's so much that needs to get done in here, and our lives are short. I'm in my forties now, and life is way too short for what we want to get done. Building a nation, or a community. It's like an orchard; it takes years for those trees to grow."

But it's like we have been on hold since 1995, and living things like a community can't be stuck like that and stay healthy.

Kevin: "Things happen. People get on with their lives, get drunk, have a fight. And then people want to hold onto that nastiness, and we can't get together and talk anymore. It's sad, really." He works on maintenance at the former army base, taking care of the old buildings and infrastructure. Summers, he spends a lot of time cutting the grass, doing what he can to take care of his homeland, inscribing and re-inscribing his claim to it in the only way he can. The roof leaks in the barracks where Kevin lives with his wife and two stepchildren, and some of the ceiling panels have fallen down.

Marcia had to leave Ipperwash soon after Melva, her mother, died. But when she tried to go back to the chapel where they had been living, the roof had leaked so much in so many places that the insulation and the ceiling panels had fallen all over the wooden floor, and the floor had started to buckle. When the chapel was struck by lightning, the power was turned off, as well as the water.

Cully has managed to stay on in the barracks she moved into back in 1995.

Cully: "This place isn't fixed up because I didn't expect to be livin' here that long. And all my grandchildren have never known me to live in a house; I'm sad about that. I mean, how many people have grandmothers that live in *barracks*?"

She spends her days in the big front room. The TV is on for all her favourite game shows. Bingo cards are clipped around the edge of a hanging stained-glass lamp emblazoned with the Coca-Cola logo. There's a dartboard on one wall, duct tape holding together pieces of the corkboard on which it's mounted, the duct tape itself multiply pierced by darts. Her work table, inset with lines for measuring, is laid out with the latest quilt she's working on: a bear-paw design in vivid red, plus black and white. She used to make beaded leatherwork and sell this too, but carpal tunnel syndrome now limits what she can do. Still, she keeps quilting – "I go nuts if I don't have something to do."

Glenn keeps a bucket and mop over by the wall where the rain comes through at one end of the Quartermaster Store where he still lives. He puts in time twisting fishnet string onto bobbins for repairing old nets while he is watching television and keeping the fire in the wood stove going. Come fall, he goes hunting and shares the meat around the community. But for how much longer?

Glenn: "I've done twenty-five years, and I'm losing interest. I don't have the juju that I had when I come in here ... I'm tired of babysittin' adults ... fuckin' drunk and carryin' on. That's what I mean. [P]eople kill themselves or kill each other. I don't like to play referee.

"But I gotta see this thing through. My priority is here."

The elders had a vision when they led us back here in the early 1990s, bringing us home. We shared it then, and still do now. We want to bring our home – the reserve – back to life. We want to bring back all our relations with each other, and with the animals and plants that live here too. We want to live all our relations with this land again. That means getting back to doing all the things we've always done on the land through all the seasons, keeping it the centre of our lives. Keeping the knowledge alive, and the stories that go with that, and the language. The feeling for what this all means to us is with us still.

Marcia: "This is where we are from, and we want to rebuild our nation in this place. We went through some hard times trying to do this, and we haven't given up."

Cully: "It's like that night when I was in jail when I had that cedar branch between me and the cops. [On the night Dudley was killed and the cops arrested and jailed Cully, a small piece of cedar got stuck on her jacket when the police pushed her down into the bushes outside the hospital. When it fell onto the floor in her jail cell, she picked it up and kept it.] And I thought, that's the Creator there saying: Even though things are *really* bad right now, it's gonna be okay. Even if it don't look like it's gonna be okay *yet*. It is gonna come around and it is gonna be okay for us where we won't have to be fightin' no more. We'll be able to practise our own ways ...

"My vision is, I would like to see [us] up and running, functioning as a reserve of our own with *all* the same stuff that *any* other reserve has."

Marcia: "I've always hoped that the community would have the recognition the same as any other reserve, any other First Nations community, where they would be able to select their own chief and council, their *own* leadership. Because the one thing that everyone would be together on is that they want the community back. They're not going to settle for selling it or getting money for it. They want it *restored.*"

Cully: "*And,* my uncle Abe always wanted to keep the maple sugar bush so we could keep making maple syrup. And I want the community centre back there so that people could go for a bush walk and see how it's done." There are plans for a cultural/community centre on the restored land here. There is even a design for a museum, drawn up by the Anishinaabe architect Douglas Cardinal.[1] Cully has been storing things, like an old black-ash woven basket, to display in the museum when it's finally built.

Glenn: "This community could go back to the way it was; kind of like a medicine community. The Cedar People used to live here. People from all over the place used to come here to get healed. You had a hard time findin' a parking spot for your canoe down there."

Kevin: "My vision is not just for our community. Our community is just one small corner of our nation. When you talk about those original agreements when they first came, when we had the two-row wampum, the proclamation, talkin' about those two boats travellin' side by side. We'll stay in ours, and you stay in yours. A sharing of the land. We never give up all of this land. We agreed to share it. We set aside small parcels where we weren't goin' to share it; that's *why* they're so small.

"This lake out here, we agreed to share it. I don't know how it's going to come about, but I know there is going to be a change. Whether it's slow or happens all at once, I don't know …

"The stepchildren I'm raising, the looks on their faces every time they hear of something movin' forward. The excitement in them! It's incredible to see, to witness. They have three lineages to Stoney Point: their mother's side, their father's side, and my side. So they're Stoney Point through and through. I try to build those kids up as much as I can because they've been through *so* much."

Bonnie: "I can't say enough thanks for those people who went in there in 1993. Those were our warriors. They weren't hoodlums or troublemakers. They were not terrorists. Glenn, Dudley, all the ones that moved there, they gave up their whole life on the outside when they did that; when they moved to Stoney Point, back home. They are fulfilling their responsibilities to our Nishnaabe way of life.

"The younger generation, they never had any pride in themselves because they only heard the worst of what happened … When our young people read this book they will be proud of the people who fought to get our land back. They'll get to read about themselves and be proud of themselves!"

Learning to Be Treaty Kin

This book is the biggest responsibility I have ever taken on as a writer. Not just because it is an important story with the moral imperative to get it right. But also because I am not the appropriate person to have been helping these Nishnaabeg tell their story. I am not Nishnaabe. I am a settler; I am a *zhaagnaash,* a "white person."

I didn't start out doubting the legitimacy of my involvement; far from it. When someone first mentioned that they'd been hoping someone with journalistic skills might show up and give them a hand pulling their stories together, I stepped right up there. I was ready to accept the implied invitation without a moment's hesitation, my privilege neatly masked by professional pride and self-confidence. The self-doubts set in only as I got more deeply involved, as I started to notice the lapsing into silence, the impatient shrug of the shoulders, the tightening of the lips. There were many awkward moments. Each one challenged me, challenged me to change. I learned to stop putting my foot in my mouth. I learned to stop myself from presuming that I as a professional writer knew best how to frame the story. By the fourth draft of the manuscript, I was getting meaningful feedback, muscular insistence that this should be phrased this way, not that. I had learned to listen deeply and respectfully enough that I could shut myself up. They took ownership where at first, when I flaunted my authorial authority, they had been inclined to defer. Gradually, I learned how to put my skills as a writer at their disposal, to step more and more into the shadows. Because by then we had formed relationships strong and rich enough that we could call each other friend if not "treaty kin."

This was key, I think. I kept coming back. I took on this work and saw it through despite the constant weight and shadow of self-doubt because I had not come here as a writer. I had not come as an observer, even a sympathetic observer. I came as a possible participant, feeling implicated in the story. I came as a settler trying to learn, however belatedly, about my treaty heritage, not just my colonial one. I had come to end my ignorance about my responsibility as a Canadian toward my treaty heritage, including how that ignorance might have contributed to the death of Dudley George in 1995.

When I first arrived outside the fence of the former Ipperwash army camp on a hot July day in 2018, ready to learn how I could share some responsibility for a broken treaty, it looked as if time had stood still since 1995. It was a palpable rendering of the price these Nishnaabeg were, and still are, paying, as justice and historical recognition continue to be essentially denied. The only new structures were some trailer units near the front gates of the former army camp, out of which the munitions-demolitions experts did their work mapping where unexploded ordnances might be. Elsewhere, there was vapour barrier on many windows of the old barracks, some of it shredding and flapping in the wind. I was told that local teenagers regularly use the unoccupied ones for weekend parties – "piss-ups" and drugs. Some front doors to the buildings where people were living did not have functioning doorknobs or locks. On most, including where Cully George and Kevin Simon still live, the shingles on the roofs were curling, cracking, and falling off. The Aazhoodena council hall, which the Nishnaabeg had built in a glorious community-reviving work bee in the summer of 1993, was in ruins, its windows broken, its roof collapsed inward, its front door permanently stuck ajar and studded with bullet holes. There were abandoned cars and trucks on the sides of the roads and in the former army camp parade ground, usually with at least two tires pancake flat, and often with grass growing up around them. There was no land-centred economy going on because the land was still being measured and marked for cleanup and still under the control of the federal government. There was a trailer facing Highway 21, rigged up as a Nishnaabe-run "Smokeshop" and another selling pot.

As I looked around the dilapidated barracks, and as I stepped up to a door, knocked, and began to meet these people, it was hard realizing how much I was part of the problem. This was clear even in the timing of when I first came, in 2018; long after the fact. I can vaguely remember having listened to the news about the unfolding standoff at Ipperwash in 1995, feeling bad when Dudley George was shot and killed, but then probably slotting it somewhere in my mind as an Indigenous issue and moving on with my life. It was hard coming here all these years later, realizing that it was my privilege that had contributed to this delay, and that I'd presumed to think that I could be the judge of when to pay attention to them; when it suited my sense of priorities, not theirs. I sat with the shame of that rather than using it as an excuse to cut and run.

I began to let go of my resistance, my fear of really listening and letting in the truth. Ironically, that helped me understand why successive governments could drag this process out, could carry on doing things according to existing budget allocations and timelines; how they could consider all of this perfectly acceptable and themselves fit to judge and determine this. Because I had arrived here still largely thinking and acting the same way. But now I could also see how convenient this was for the status quo, how it allowed the status quo to carry on.

I no longer see this as acceptable.

Justice demands honouring the things to which this country, in recent steps toward historical reparation, has committed and recommitted itself. It demands that we honour Section 35 of the 1982 Canadian Constitution and its Charter of Rights and Freedoms as well as the UN Declaration on the Rights of Indigenous Peoples, to which, through Bill C-15, adopted in 2021, the Canadian Government has committed itself. Justice demands that we honour the changed public realities flowing from Supreme Court judgments, including the 1997 *Delgamuukw* decision, and historical research challenging the "cede and surrender" clause written into so many treaty documents accompanying the settler colonization of the country.[1]

Justice demands unsettling the status quo. And this requires ceding and surrendering the colonial mindset.

That mindset haunts the Ipperwash tragedy like a devouring ghost – starting with the presumption to take over the entire Stoney Point Reserve in the first place, not because that site was essential but because it was convenient. It continues through to the minister of National Defence sending a general to Kettle Point in 1993 to explain to the elders who had gone to reclaim their ancestral homeland at

Stoney Point why the army still needed that land "into the foresee-able future." It carries on in the Ontario Provincial Police thinking they had adequately consulted as long as they had talked with the Indian Act band council chief and in their preparing briefing notes acknowledging the colour of right but in their actions not recognizing this colour, not respecting the treaty justification for this sense of being in the right.

Racialized and overtly racist ways of thinking dovetailed with colonial ones from the beginning ("a few straggling Indians") and continued to do so throughout the unfolding drama. They were espe-cially evident in the massive police buildup at Ipperwash and the firing of that fatal bullet. The two worked hand in hand in govern-ment meetings on September 5 and 6, 1995, in what was said (liken-ing the ancestral land-claiming Nishnaabeg to Hells Angels bikers) and what was muted or not said at all. The possibility of a peaceful resolution through negotiation mandated by the Ontario Inter-Ministerial Committee on Aboriginal Emergencies was never even discussed, tacitly overshadowed and overruled by a strictly law en-forcement approach to the latest manifestation of "the Indian prob-lem," as it was framed in the 1850s and '60s.

Denial is a tough habit to break, perhaps because it operates on a personal as well as a public level, through official gatekeepers like government ministers who will invite certain people into their of-fices, recognizing their status and authority, or not. Denial as pat-terns of disassociation can be so subtle they are hard to even see because the filters at work are invisible.

Much as I resisted, I could identify with the Ontario government bureaucrats who might have prevented Dudley George's death if they had spoken up – or pushed harder when they did. I recall one moment in particular. This was at a September 5 meeting of the Inter-Ministerial Committee on Aboriginal Emergencies when Jeff Bangs, the executive assistant to the Ontario minister of Natural Resources, mentioned the policy document created by the previous (NDP) government called Statement of Political Relationship. This policy, a rehearsal of Bill C-15 regarding the United Nations Declaration on the Rights of Indigenous Peoples in a way, called for all provincial government relations with First Nations to be respectful of treaty relationships and to recognize First Nations' inherent right to self-government. Although Bangs urged the committee to be mindful of this as a guide, his suggestion was merely noted in passing. This line of thinking did not have enough currency or traction in the room – not enough people felt implicated in forging that relationship – to push the discussion in a new, more post- and anticolonial direction. Instead, the assimilating notion that all people living in Canada are individuals first and foremost and are to be treated equally carried the day.

It could have been me at that meeting, possibly feeling virtuous that I had at least tried, but unable to dislodge the centuries-old colonial thinking or challenge the strictly law-and-order perspective that prevailed. Not now though.

The journey of this book has challenged me to change my mind and sense of priorities and taught me how important it is to do so. It has forced me to see some of my hidden (even from myself) assumptions, to take responsibility for them and how they help perpetuate an unjust status quo. It has compelled me to struggle to set these aside and thus participate in changing the status quo; though this is far easier said than done! Yet, as I succeeded in at least starting to do this, as I started to cede and surrender space in my own mind and imagination, I found myself open to new learning and the possibilities this has offered.

That is the unexpected gift that I have received by taking up the challenge these Nishnaabe women and men put to me four years ago: to help them tell their story in their own words, from their perspective. I took on the work of recording and transcribing their stories, editing them together, wordsmithing possible narrative links and generally being their storytelling helper, pro bono. I did it not out of settler guilt but from a sense of accountability. I wanted to learn how to be accountable to a settler heritage that includes the Indigenous tradition of treaty making and renewal. I wanted to serve and support the coming together of their story as this book and have done this in the spirit of condolences and reparations – the necessary preliminaries to even the possibility of a renewed treaty relationship: settler and First Nation.

I hope to give back, to reciprocate the gifts of learning I have received from Bonnie, Cully, Marcia, Janet, Marlin, Kevin, Glenn, Maynard, Gina, Joy, and others. Perhaps I can join a settler counternarrative, even contribute to it, and help bring this to the treaty table, on every level of imagining a treaty table taking shape – from the political to the institutional, to the cultural and the personal.

I will share some of this learning and these thoughts in a memoir I am writing as this book goes to press. Meanwhile, I hope my shift in thinking might help place me on the healing path that RoseAnne Archibald, grand chief of the Assembly of First Nations, talks about, because I consider what I am doing to be a healing – and very much ongoing. It has also caused me to withdraw my consent to be governed by the kind of policies that produced the Ipperwash tragedy and have perpetuated it by ongoing neglect and delay. I hope others will make a similar decision and will engage in a similar struggle, first inwardly and then outwardly, determined to rectify centuries of wrongdoing to the Indigenous Peoples of this land, and see justice finally done.

Heather Menzies

Notes

Introduction

1 John Borrows is the author of many books, chapters in books, and scholarly articles in which he elaborates this argument and its basis in historical fact.

2 One of Canada's leading non-Indigenous historians, Peter Russell, does appreciate it. He also regards William Johnson, who facilitated the treaty making at Niagara in 1764, as a first Father of Confederation. See Peter Russell, *Canada's Odyssey: A Country Based on Incomplete Conquests* (Toronto: University of Toronto Press, 2017), 51.

3 John Borrows, *Canada's Indigenous Constitution* (Toronto: University of Toronto Press, 2010), 21.

4 Ibid., 24.

5 Ibid., 24

6 Ibid., 28.

7 Robin Wall Kimmerer, *Braiding Sweetgrass: Indigenous Wisdom, Scientific Knowledge and the Teachings of Plants* (Minneapolis: Milkweed Editions, 2013), 157.

8 Lisa Brooks, *Our Beloved Kin: A New History of King Philip's War* (New Haven: Yale University Press, 2018), 21.

9 Ibid., 19.

10 Borrows, *Canada's Indigenous Constitution*, 26.

11 Borrows, *Recovering Canada: The Resurgence of Indigenous Law* (Toronto: University of Toronto Press, 2002), 125. These principles include recognition of Aboriginal self-governance, free trade, affirmation of Aboriginal consent in treaty matters, respect for hunting and fishing rights, and adherence to principles of peace and friendship.

12 Brooks, *Our Beloved Kin*, 21.

13 Lisa Brooks, *The Common Pot* (Minneapolis: University of Minnesota Press, 2008), 151 and 157. This understanding also derived from John Borrows' writing.

14 This responsibility is also named in the 1996 Report of the Royal Commission on Aboriginal Peoples, Volume 1 – Looking Forward, Looking Back, 120: "In the tradition of Indian nations, treaties are not merely between governments. They are made between nations, and every individual member of the allied nations assumes personal responsibility for respecting the treaty."

15 Emery Shawwanoo Bigknife, "Kettle Point History of Families: Our Oshawanoo Roots." Family document produced by author (2003).

16 The forced removal of the Cherokee is known as "Trail of Tears," but for the Potawatomi it is known as the "Trail of Death."

17 This is how Ojibway-Anishinaabe Jerry Fontaine translates the word in *Our Hearts Are as One Fire* (Vancouver: UBC Press, 2020). It is also listed as the original (if "obsolete") meaning in Richard A. Rhodes, *Eastern Ojibwa-Chippewa-Ottawa Dictionary*. The elders of Nawash and Saugeen First Nation translate the word as "the good of the earth" or "good beings." Quoted in David McLaren's paper, "Under Siege" prepared for the Ipperwash Inquiry, December 2005.

18 One of those who carried on living on the land was Abraham George's son Stewart ("Worm"). He died of cancer in 2020.

CHAPTER 1: NO WORD FOR SURRENDER

1 Clifford George died during the course of the Ipperwash Inquiry. These quotes are drawn mostly from his witness testimony at the Inquiry, supplemented by some other unpublished records.

2 All the quotes from Rose Manning are also taken from her witness testimony at the Inquiry.

3 Fontaine, *Our Hearts Are as One Fire*, 8.

4 Ibid.

5 "History of the Anishinabek Nation," https://www.anishinabek.ca/who-we-are-and-what-we-do/.

6 Peter S. Schmalz, *The Ojibwa of Southern Ontario* (Toronto: University of Toronto Press, 1991), 14–16.

7 John Borrows, "Wampum at Niagara," in *Aboriginal and Treaty Rights in Canada*, ed. Michael Asch (Vancouver: UBC Press, 1997), 160. As Borrows explained its contradiction: "its wording recognized Aboriginal rights to land by outlining a policy that was designed to extinguish these rights."

8 Ibid., 46.

9 Borrows, *Recovering Canada*, 125.

10 Quoted in ibid.

11 Borrows, "Wampum at Niagara," 161, n 58.

12 Ibid., 161.

13 This is how Johnson put it in a letter to his superiors in December, 1763. John Borrows, "Niagara Treaty Records" (unpublished, on file with author), 9.

14 Borrows, "Wampum at Niagara," 163.

15 He did follow English tradition by distributing a commemorative medal. It was inscribed around the edge with the date, 1764, and the words "Happy While

United," and its face depicted two men, British and Anishinaabe, sitting under a tree smoking a long peace pipe, with a fire (possibly the treaty council fire) in the background.

16 Alan Ojiig Corbiere, "'Their Own Forms of Which They Take The Most Notice': Diplomatic Metaphors and Symbolism on Wampum Belts," in *Anishinaabewin Niiwin: Four Rising Winds,* ed. Alan Ojiig Corbiere, Mary Ann Naokwegijig Corbiere, Deborah McGregor, and Crystal Migwans (M'Chigeeng, ON: Ojibwe Cultural Foundation, 2014), 58.

17 Borrows, "Wampum at Niagara," 164.

18 Corbiere, "'Their Own Forms,'" 49.

19 Scholars such as Borrows and Corbiere strongly suspect that the respected Mohawk matron Molly Brant, who was Johnson's consort and the mother of their children, would have arranged for these belts to be made.

20 Borrows, "Wampum at Niagara," 163.

21 Corbiere, "'Their Own Forms,'" 62. Corbiere learned this from Ken Maracle, a Mohawk wampum belt maker, who in turn had been told this by an elder.

22 Corbiere, "'Their Own Forms,'" 63. And personal communication (Alan Ojiig Corbiere, email to Heather Menzies, October 22, 2021).

23 Borrows, "Wampum at Niagara," 161. Borrows notes that by extending the convention of the covenant chain of friendship in that belt, Johnson signalled that "a multination alliance in which no member gave up their sovereignty, was affirmed" at Niagara.

24 Corbiere, "'Their Own Forms,'" 63.

25 Borrows, "Wampum at Niagara," 164.

26 Ibid., 50.

27 Russell, *Canada's Odyssey,* 78.

28 Schmalz, *Ojibwa of Southern Ontario,* 111.

29 Jordan George, "KSPFN Community/Historical Timeline 1750–1827." Stapled document produced by KSPFN band office.

30 G. Elmore Reaman, *The Trail of the Black Walnut* (Baltimore, ML: Genealogical Publishing, 1993).

31 Schmalz, *Ojibwa of Southern Ontario,* 124.

32 Ibid., 125.

33 Robert J. Surtees, *Indian Land Surrenders in Ontario, 1763–1867* (Ottawa: Indian and Northern Affairs Canada, 1983), 80–85. This also fits our own oral histories.

34 Darlene Johnston, *Connecting People to Place: Great Lakes Aboriginal History in Cultural Context.* Research report for Ipperwash Inquiry (2007), 22.

35 Darlene Johnston, *Respecting and Protecting the Sacred.* Research report for Ipperwash Inquiry (2007), 5.

36 Johnston uses the spelling most historians have followed, calling him Wapagace. However, his name meant "small piece of clay," and we have chosen to follow the spelling in Richard A. Rhodes' *Eastern Ojibwa-Chippewa-Ottawa Dictionary* (Berlin: Mouton de Gruyter, 1993): *Waabgan* means "clay" and the suffix *aans* means "small." In writing our language, the letters *p* and *b* are often used interchangeably.

37 Johnston, *Connecting People to Place,* 4.
38 Nishnaabemowin, like many Indigenous languages, distinguishes between animate and inanimate but not between male and female. This gender distinction was part of Perrot's account.
39 Johnston, *Respecting and Protecting the Sacred,* 4.
40 Ibid., 5.
41 Johnston, *Connecting People to Place,* 7.
42 Ibid., 25.
43 Johnston, *Respecting and Protecting the Sacred,* 6.
44 Quoted in ibid., 9.
45 Quoted in Johnston, *Connecting People to Place,* 22.
46 Edward Shortt, ed., *Perth Remembered* (Perth: Perth Museum, 1967); Michael Gonder Scherck, *Pen Pictures of Early Pioneer Life in Upper Canada* (Toronto: William Briggs, 1905); Catherine Parr Traill, *The Canadian Emigrant Housekeeper's Guide* (Toronto: Lovell & Gibson, 1862).
47 According to research done for the Ipperwash Inquiry by Joan Holmes, this promise was not included in the final text of the treaty. Ipperwash Inquiry (Ont.) and Sidney B. Linden, *Report of the Ipperwash Inquiry* (Toronto: Ministry of the Attorney General, Queen's Printer for Ontario, 2007), 1:29.
48 Surtees, *Indian Land Surrenders in Ontario, 1763–1867,* 80.
49 Russell, *Canada's Odyssey,* 89.
50 Bob Joseph, *21 Things You May Not Know about the Indian Act* (Port Coquitlam: Indigenous Relations Press, 2018), 27.
51 Ibid., 28.
52 Canada's first prime minister, "Sir" John A. Macdonald, told parliament that Canada's role was "to do away with the tribal system and assimilate the Indian people in all respects with the inhabitants of the Dominion." Quoted in Ipperwash Inquiry and Linden, *Report of the Ipperwash Inquiry* 1:34.
53 Ipperwash Inquiry and Linden, *Report of the Ipperwash Inquiry* 1:40.
54 Holmes quoted in Ipperwash Inquiry and Linden, *Report of the Ipperwash Inquiry* 1:41.
55 Quoted in Ipperwash Inquiry and Linden, *Report of the Ipperwash Inquiry,* 44.
56 This is beautifully described by Potawatomi botanist and academic Robin Wall Kimmerer in *Braiding Sweetgrass,* 145.

CHAPTER 2: "THE HOUSE WAS GONE"

1 Although our land is collectively owned and shared, individual families have use rights to a certain amount of land that, like private property, can be inherited and even sold – but only to someone else on the reserve. Generally, a family would have forty acres for living and additional land in the bush for cutting timber and firewood.
2 The government had our land formally assessed at the time because, apparently, they initially intended to buy the reserve outright. They assessed it at fifteen dollars an acre, which is what we used when "selling" land to each other on the reserve.

3 Helen Roos, "It Happened as if Overnight: The Expropriation and Relocation of Stoney Point Reserve #43, 1942" (master's thesis, University of Western Ontario, 1998), as quoted in Ipperwash Inquiry and Linden, *Report of the Ipperwash Inquiry* 1:55.

Chapter 3: Disruption and Determination

1 From Clifford George's witness testimony at the Ipperwash Inquiry.
2 The act gave the government the authority to terminate people's status as Indians if they graduated from university, served in the Armed Forces, or left the reserve for long periods, possibly for work. It was rescinded in 1985.
3 There were many others who were also enfranchised. It made things difficult when we returned to Stoney Point because they were no longer entitled to the land their families had lived on for generations.
4 McLaren, "Under Siege," 14.
5 The order-in-council went on to say that when the army no longer needed the land, "negotiations would then be entered into to transfer the same land back to the Indians at a reasonable price to be determined by mutual agreement." This confirmed what some people had suspected all along: that the government had tried to pull a fast one on us, trying to swindle us out of our treaty-protected homeland.
6 Many of us are descended from Oshawanoo.

Chapter 4: Under Cover of Prayer Meetings

1 This was rescinded, but only in 1951.
2 Johnston and Holmes quoted in Ipperwash Inquiry and Linden, *Report of the Ipperwash Inquiry* 1:30.
3 Ipperwash Inquiry and Linden, *Report of the Ipperwash Inquiry* 1:62.
4 Joseph Schull, *Ontario since 1867* (Toronto: McClelland and Stewart, 1978), 345, 353.
5 Ipperwash Inquiry and Linden, *Report of the Ipperwash Inquiry* 1:64.

Chapter 5: Burying the Hatchet under a Peace Tree

1 Peter Edwards, *One Dead Indian: The Premier, the Police, and the Ipperwash Crisis* (Toronto: McClelland and Stewart, 2001), 61.
2 "Acting" because we had decided to hold off on having elections until we were back at Stoney. Also, Carl George changed his name to Tolsma in 1997. But we are leaving the name he used when we were all together then.
3 Some people also call it the Prayer Tree; they hang tobacco ties from the branches.
4 This was likely an emergency tracheotomy to help Abe breathe. He was then taken to hospital and stayed there for six months.
5 In fact, Stoney Point never lost its legal status as a reserve.

Chapter 6: Peacekeepers and Nation Builders

1 Taiaiake Alfred and Lana Lowe, *Warrior Societies in Contemporary Indigenous Communities*. Research paper for Ipperwash Inquiry (2005), 5.
2 This was likely on the way home, since Tyendinaga is along the St. Lawrence River and the 401 Highway.
3 Karen Hawthorne, "Long Walk with a Message," *Kitchener-Waterloo Record,* September 16, 1993, B1.
4 When Dudley was seventeen and in Grade 10, he was one of a group of teens who set fire to a lumberyard warehouse in Forest. He was the only Indigenous youth in the group and the only one to be jailed – for twenty-one months for arson – despite his school principal appealing to the judge, describing Dudley as honest, reliable, and hard-working and saying: "I believe in this young man." Edwards, *One Dead Indian,* 57.

Chapter 7: Taking the Barracks

1 Quoted in Ipperwash Inquiry and Linden, *Report of the Ipperwash Inquiry* 1:3.
2 We never knew what that was all about. We were not even sure he was from the *Globe and Mail.* Lots of people would show up claiming they were from this media or that. Just snooping sometimes, we thought.
3 A flare type of firecracker that spits sparkles.

Chapter 8: September 5–6, 1995, Project Maple

1 All of the detailed information and quotes in this chapter are drawn from Justice Linden's Ipperwash Report and the witness transcripts.
2 Quoted in Ipperwash Inquiry and Linden, *Report of the Ipperwash Inquiry* 1:137.
3 Ipperwash Inquiry and Linden, *Report of the Ipperwash Inquiry* 1:618.
4 The Conservative Party had stated its position clearly in election documents like "A Voice for the North," promising that if Mike Harris was elected premier, he would treat everyone equally under the law. This told Gordon Peters, who was Regional Chief for the Chiefs of Ontario, that "They're going to step up their processes of assimilation. They're going to try to bring us into the mainstream. It means they're going to disregard our treaty relationships and ... virtually revert back to the 1969 White Paper that set out a process about how ... Indigenous peoples would be swallowed up within the politic of Canada." Ipperwash Inquiry and Linden, *Report of the Ipperwash Inquiry* 1:116–17.
5 Quoted in Edwards, *One Dead Indian,* 68.
6 In his Ipperwash Inquiry report, Justice Sidney B. Linden made it clear that this direct communication of operational information between Fox and Carson was inappropriate. Ipperwash Inquiry and Linden, *Report of the Ipperwash Inquiry* 4:52.
7 Ipperwash Inquiry and Linden, *Report of the Ipperwash Inquiry* 1:277.
8 In fact, at the time, none of the Crowd Management Unit (CMU) had been deployed and no decision had been made to deploy them.

Chapter 10: After the Shooting

1 Edwards, *One Dead Indian,* 132.
2 Carson's version of what happened was mostly what the media reported. But it was untrue.
3 Its full name at the time was Indian Affairs and Northern Development. It was subsequently modified to Indigenous Affairs.
4 Ipperwash Inquiry and Linden, *Report of the Ipperwash Inquiry* 1:618.

Epilogue: Two Boats Travelling Side by Side

1 Douglas Cardinal was raised in Blackfoot Territory.

Afterword: Learning to Be Treaty Kin

1 It has become clear that the treaty documents were not a faithful record of what was negotiated and agreed to in the face-to-face negotiations. In treaty after treaty, it has been shown that the Indigenous parties agreed to share the land, not to cede and surrender it. See, for example, Sheldon Krasowski, *No Surrender: The Land Remains Indigenous* (Regina: University of Regina Press, 2019).

Index

Printed and bound in Canada by Friesens

Set in Garamond and Charis by Artegraphica Design Co.

Copy editor: Candida Hadley

Proofreader: Alison Strobel

Indexer: Judy Dunlop

Cartographer: Eric Leinberger

Cover designer: George Kirkpatrick

Cover image:
Dudley George's great-niece and -nephew, Jana and Aidan,
walking near Lake Huron in their traditional territory,
wearing regailia that was made and beaded by their grandmother,
Carolyn (Cully) George Mandoka. Photograph by Racheal Manidoka